"Peter Som's recipes are stunningly imaginative, chic, and sure to bring joy to your dining room table. Heritage, tradition, and modernity are seen through his unique lens, and I for one am excited to dive in. *Family Style* is an essential book for every cook's library."

—ANGIE MAR, chef/founder, Mar Hospitality Group

"Peter Som has created something truly original in *Family Style*—there were so many times I shouted, 'Why didn't I think of that?' I want to cook everything in this book."

—RUTH REICHL, *New York Times* bestselling author of *The Paris Novel* and *Save Me the Plums*

FAMILY STYLE

Turkey Meatballs with Corn,
Stone Fruit, and Sumac
Labneh (page 158)

FAMILY STYLE

Elegant Everyday Recipes
Inspired by Home and Heritage

PETER SOM

Photographs by Linda Xiao

HARVEST
An Imprint of WILLIAM MORROW

HarperCollins books may be purchased for educational, business, or sales promotional use. For information, please email the Special Markets Department at SPsales@harpercollins.com.

FIRST EDITION

Photographer: Linda Xiao
Food Stylist: Sue Li
Prop Stylist: Sarah Smart
Editor: Sarah Kwak
Designer: Melissa Lotfy
Copy Editor: Karen Wise

Library of Congress Cataloging-in-Publication Data

Names: Som, Peter, author.

Title: Family style : elegant everyday recipes inspired by home and heritage / Peter Som ; photographs by Linda Xiao.

Description: First edition. | New York, NY : Harvest, an imprint of William Morrow, [2025] | Includes index. | Identifiers: LCCN 2024033438 | ISBN 9780063347304 (hardcover) | ISBN 9780063347311 (ebook)

Subjects: LCSH: Cooking. | LCGFT: Cookbooks.

Classification: LCC TX714 .S6155 2025 | DDC 641.5—dc23/eng/20240907

LC record available at https://lccn.loc.gov/2024033438

ISBN 978-0-06-334730-4

25 26 27 28 29 cos 10 9 8 7 6 5 4 3 2 1

To Helen and Mary

Mom and her mom—my grandma Mary—are the two people in my life who have influenced and imprinted their love of food onto my heart, my soul, and my stomach. Their interest in cooking may have been born out of obvious necessity to feed their families, but that frisson of excitement, that spark of a smile when talking about food—that was about love, and wanting to do everything and more to bring everyone to the table. Because once the table was set, and the platters of food were set out, and the rice cooker finished, there was nothing more important than sitting down together and breaking bread—or in our case, filling our rice bowls.

For them, anything worth doing meant giving it your very best effort. That meant methodically picking out each pea pod before placing it in a bag, making sure they got the leanest piece of char siu with the right amount of char and caramelization (and not too much fat, m'goy la!), and driving out of their way to buy the perfect bao. My grandma passed away more than twenty years ago, but her memory lives with me each time I turn on the fire under my wok or chop scallions.

Helen and Mary. Two women whose experiences, journeys, and lives have informed my cooking and my approach to food—and life. This book is for both of you.

Contents

Recipes

Intro-
duction

"Have you eaten?"

That was always how Grandma greeted me when I stepped into her apartment. Sometimes it was a voice from the kitchen, rising above the singsong of the rice cooker and the hum of the stove fan. Other times it was heard through the muffle of her enveloping hug. Her second greeting—whether or not I'd had time to recount my food intake up to that point in the day—was "Are you hungry? (Tow m'tow ngo?)" Then finally, a hello and a quick grandmotherly assessment of my hair and my face. Amid the adult bustle of my parents taking off coats, discussing where we parked, the inspection of some Very Nice Oranges that were brought over, I would pass by the large sliding glass doors that framed the usually foggy San Francisco Bay and scoot into the galley kitchen alone. There, I'd gingerly lift a lid and inhale the elixir of simmering Chinese mushrooms. I'd peek into the fridge to see the fat leaves of bok choy peeking out of brown bags, waiting to be sautéed. I'd spy Grandma's well-worn Chinese cleaver on the cutting board next to slices of ginger and scallions—the peppery aroma hitting my nose that, when I was a kid, was perfectly at counter height.

"Would someone go to Clement Street because Mei Wa Market has really good gai lan—especially good this week."

"And don't forget the pea shoots. How much do we need? They looked so fresh!"

"What time is dim sum at Yank Sing?" Noon? Oh good, we can also buy some extra char siu bao—they are so good. We should bring some to Auntie Bernie, she loves them."

"Auntie Gloria is bringing dessert— oh, can't wait!—it's some sort of torte."

"Don't forget to get yuk sung for jook tomorrow, we already got yàuhjagwái from that place off of Grant Avenue. What was it called?"

For as long as I can remember, food—the discussion of it, the making of it, the eating of it, the *everything* of it—has been central to my life. A running joke in our family is that we always talk about our next meal at the present meal. At lunch? The conversation would inevitably meander to dinner, which would be brought up like very important talking points at a board meeting.

When I was growing up, meals always consisted of large shared platters all set in the middle of the table.

So, my favorite way to eat? Always family style.

My fondness for family style meals has evolved as I started to connect with my own cooking and what it means to me. Family style has become the gathering of family—whether blood or chosen—to create and experience a meal together. A few glasses of wine, some '80s music playing, maybe a bit of dancing about. But family style goes beyond the meal itself. When I'm home in my New York City kitchen cooking, I'm not alone. When I start chopping scallions or rinsing rice, I like to think I'm surrounded by—and cooking with—those who love me. I'm cooking with Grandma when I make her perfect apple cake (see page 204). I'm with Mom when I'm making her soy sauce chicken (and quite often FaceTiming her to ask her a question about an ingredient or to confirm a cook time).

Family style is also about bringing out that individuality and that touch of flair that's unique to everyone. For me, cooking is about creativity, trusting your instincts, and taking risks with flavors, and *Family Style* will introduce you to new flavor combinations to inspire your own magic in the kitchen. Charred broccoli is dressed in chili crisp and honey *and* showered with parmesan (page 59). My mochi blondies are infused with miso *and* brown butter (page 226). The flavors of cacio e pepe mingle with steamed sticky rice (page 90). The act of cooking and presenting a meal is the greatest act of love, and always an opportunity to showcase style. As I've been in the fashion and

design world for a long time, it's second nature for me to make sure that my dishes have curb appeal. But style shouldn't be belabored. It can be as easy as adding a flourish of herbs, a drizzle of olive oil, or the finishing sprinkle of flaky sea salt. This shouldn't be reserved for special occasions!

Whether you're making something on the fly to enjoy solo or preparing a dinner for eight, feeding oneself and those closest to you is—for me—a joy. That's what *Family Style* is about. So, this book is for all of us who favor a flavor chase and are always up for an adventure, no matter where it takes us—and hopefully it will help you in unleashing your own creativity in the kitchen, to tap into your own food memories and fearlessly bring them into the now, and make them truly *you*, so you can share them—family style—with those you love.

THE FAMILY STYLE WAY

In Chinese culture, meals are fun to be sure, but not a casual free-for-all. There's a distinct etiquette that Mom and Grandma taught me as a kid, especially at large dinners out at the family's favorite restaurants, and I still abide by these rules to this day. They will serve you well, whether you're sharing a few plates with friends at your favorite West Village Italian restaurant (Via Carota, for me) or at a table of 14 for a 15-course Chinese banquet.

First of all, *calm down*. You will get your helping. OK, now here are the rules:

TAKE ONLY A SMALL PORTION.
There will be more the second time around on the lazy Susan.

TAKE ONLY THE FOOD CLOSEST TO YOU ON THE PLATTER.
(Don't go reaching to the far end of the platter fishing around for that perfect piece of squab!)

USE SERVING SPOONS.
Always. Unless you're dining with your nearest and dearest—in which case it might be OK using your own chopsticks to select your food from the platter. (My mom would like to go on the record that serving spoons should be used all of the time.) But please, only touch what you're taking.

SERVE THOSE NEXT TO YOU FIRST.
Especially if you're sitting next to your elders—Grandma or Auntie So-and-So—though they will object and invariably start serving you or telling you to just serve yourself, in which case you may relent.

AS MUCH AS YOU LOVE THAT CRISPY ORANGE BEEF AND BROCCOLI, RESIST THE URGE TO TAKE THE LAST PIECE FROM THE PLATTER.
You should offer it to someone else or offer it to Grandma, who will hopefully say, "Ayyiah, I'm too full—you take it."

Now, let's dig in, shall we?

DINNER AT . . . WAIT!

Hold up! How many people are coming over for dinner? Don't stress. Having hosted many a dinner party over the years, from impromptu lunches for 2 to Thanksgiving for 30—I've gotten things down to a secondhand science. So, let's get down to numbers. And what I always say is . . .

1. KEEP IT SIMPLE.

This is the golden rule, people. For the food, the drinks, and the table.

2. TABLE IT.

Unless you're a Martha-level crafter, keep the table simple. My go-to? A tablecloth or, even better, a runner, because they're smaller and easier to clean and iron. I'm a big fan of deli flower bouquets, taken apart/rearranged in bud vases placed down the table (pro tip: odd numbers look better). Make sure your flowers are chin height so everyone can see their dining companions.

3. DIM ALL THE LIGHTS, SWEET DARLING.

Ditch or dim the overhead lighting and use candles or table lamps for a flattering vibe. Think about your favorite restaurant or cocktail lounge and imitate that mood. Everybody looks better by candlelight—I buy votives by the bag at IKEA. I mean nobody wants to dine in CVS-level fluorescents, am I right?

4. FOCUS, FOCUS!

You're not the buffet at the Delta Lounge, so there's no need to try to make a raft of dishes to satisfy every guest. Focus on 3 or 4 dishes. A starter (salad is always a good option), a main, a grain or starch, and then dessert. Try to prepare as much as possible beforehand—whether something is fully made and only needs to be reheated, or everything is washed, chopped, and ready to go. The pros call it mise en place. Within those chosen dishes, think of it as a Broadway cast—one dish is the star (usually the main course) and might take more work, the next two supporting cast members are easier (either prepared ahead of time, can be served room temperature, or assembled at the last minute), and the last one is the chorus (this one is either bought at the bakery or grocery store or brought by a guest).

5. HELP, I NEED SOMEBODY!

If friends offer to bring something or to help, let them. Ask someone to bring something sweet if you're not up to baking. However, I'm a fan of putting a plate down on the table with some hunks of very good chocolate, or a bowl of very good in-season fruit. Not necessary but always nice: If you have an extra-large dinner party and you're able to, hire someone who can assist with clearing dishes and making drinks. You'll enjoy the evening a lot more knowing the dishwasher will be running and the kitchen will be clean at the end of the night.

What's in My Pantry

I love a list because it makes me feel organized when I so often feel decidedly unorganized. Here's a list of ingredients that I turn to on the regular, so on a Tuesday at 6:45 p.m. I can run into my kitchen and turn out a pretty delicious meal by just grabbing a few of these flavor bombs. Combine with pasta or chicken, some veg, or maybe a few eggs (I love eggs for dinner) and you're done. Some are big on umami, others are evergreen basics, but all are indispensable for pulling a meal together—and I've probably used most of them in combination with each other (yes, even Pecorino Romano and soy sauce) over the years.

ON THE COUNTERTOP

My beyond-essentials? Right here! I keep these guys right next to the stove for quick, easy access. Put them on the side of the stove of your dominant hand (left, for this leftie). This little group is what I use in pretty much all of my cooking.

Extra-Virgin Olive Oil

Flaky Sea Salt

Freshly Ground Black Pepper

Kosher Salt: I prefer Diamond Crystal.

Local Honey: My go-to when I need a touch of sweetness.

Neutral Oil: For stir-fries and other high-heat cooking, neutral oils with a mild flavor and a high smoke point like grapeseed oil or avocado oil are a must.

IN THE FRIDGE

My refrigerator door is home to an array of flavor-packed ingredients that shorten the time between cooking and stuffing my face.

Anchovy Paste: The stuff in the tube saves time on chopping up whole anchovies, and you can use as little or as much as you want.

Butter (European-style, please): European-style butter has a higher butterfat content and less water—for us that means richer and more flavorful butter. All recipes in this book use unsalted butter, but I do enjoy salted butter on toast, so I keep a few sticks of those on hand as well in the fridge (with backups in the freezer).

Capers: Chopped or left whole, capers are the perfect shortcut to that briny depth of flavor for sauces, vegetables, and pasta.

Chili Crisp: Instant big flavor here! Heat, texture, sweetness. Chili crisp is an ingredient, condiment, and dip and is the main event in my Parm Broccoli with Honey Chili Crisp (page 59). Fly By Jing is one of my favorite brands.

Dijon Mustard: Truly a go-to and a staple for its distinctive tang, creaminess, and overall versatility. Maille is my go-to.

Fish Sauce: You'll find that a splash of this deep, funky Southeast and East Asian sauce will liven up vinaigrettes, stews, and sauces. I use nước chấm—Vietnamese-style fish sauce—like Red Boat.

Fresh Herbs: I always have a handful of fresh herbs in my fridge—wrapped in a paper towel and stored in a zip-top bag. They bring instant brightness to any dish and are often the finishing touch to make a plate of food feel that much more special. The selection rotates seasonally, but you'll always find flat-leaf parsley, thyme, and scallions (technically not an herb, but I use them in very much the same way).

Ginger: The fresh kind. Like my grandma and mom, I never peel ginger (though you're free to).

Gochujang: Sweet heat, thy name is gochujang. One of my most-used ingredients in the kitchen, and a key component in my swicy (that's sweet + spicy!) sauce (page 9).

Greek Yogurt: Tang and creaminess? It's here.

Harissa Paste: This North African and Middle Eastern spice paste brings equal parts heat, spice, and fragrance to every step of cooking.

Hoisin Sauce: One of my top go-to's! Hoisin's rich, deep BBQ-adjacent flavor profile brings instant umami to meats, vegetables, sauces, and so much more, as in my Hoisin Honey Roast Chicken (page 155).

Kewpie Mayonnaise: A rich Japanese-style mayonnaise that's made with egg yolks. It's velvety, creamy, and more flavorful than regular mayo. Once you try it, you'll be hooked. Case in point, my Oeufs Kewpie (page 2).

Labneh: This soft Middle Eastern strained cheese is made from yogurt that's creamy, thick, and rich—perfect for a quick sauce. Greek yogurt can be used instead if you can't find labneh at your grocery store.

Lemons and Limes: My everyday pick for a bright hit of acid to make food sing—whether the juice or zest (or both), whether added during cooking or as a final touch to the finished dish. I always have a handful of each in my fridge.

Maple Syrup: For caramelized depth of flavor—it'll sweeten up any marinade, dressing, or sauce.

Miso: There are many types of miso with varying ranges of flavor intensity, but I always have white or yellow miso on hand for its versatility. I add it to everything from desserts to sauces to soups.

Oyster Sauce: Part of the sweet, salty, umami crew and perfect for sauces, stir-fries, and marinades.

Parmigiano-Reggiano: A nutty, almost sweet flavor that we all know and love. Also, save the rinds! They add depth of flavor to soups and stocks.

Pecorino Romano: Salty, bright, and tangy. This Italian beauty is the perfect finish to almost any savory dish. Try it in my Udon with Charred Sardines and Pecorino (page 98).

Sriracha: Sweet heat lives here.

Tomato Paste in a Tube: So much better than the can when you need only a tablespoon or two.

Whole-Grain Mustard: Usually used in tandem with its smoother pal Dijon, this one brings the texture.

IN THE FREEZER

Chicken Stock: It seems I constantly have a zip-top bag of chicken carcasses from meals past in the freezer—all for the reason to make homemade stock, which I store in quart containers, ready for whenever the soup, stew, or sauce urge hits.

Flour: Yep, I keep flour in the freezer, as it extends shelf life.

Peas: A must! (As I'm probably not shelling fresh peas anytime soon.)

Puff Pastry: For instant, fancy-ish desserts and toppers to things like my One Big Seafood Pot Pie (page 132).

IN THE PANTRY

Balsamic Vinegar: Sweet-tart and full of caramel notes.

Cannellini Beans: Creamy, dreamy white beans for dips, soups, and my Fancy Mushrooms and Creamy Beans with Citrus Brown Butter (page 75).

Chickpeas: A quick, healthy add to any meal.

Golden Raisins: The perfect sweet finishing touch to salads, roasted vegetables, and fish.

Nuts (toasted, unsalted): I keep walnuts, almonds, and pistachios on hand for snacking and for that finishing crunch to a dish.

Panko Breadcrumbs: For shatteringly crisp coatings as well as a crunchy finish for salads and pastas, or in my Panko Salmon with Labneh Dijonnaise (page 123).

Pasta and Noodles: A few boxes will do. My favorites are bucatini and paccheri, along with ramen and soba. This way I can make my Easy Roasted Garlic Pasta (page 105) at a moment's notice.

Rice and Grains: I stock jasmine and arborio rice, as well as farro.

Rice Wine Vinegar: A gentle acidity and sweet flavor vibe live here for vinaigrettes, pickling, and more.

Soy Sauce: The backbone of most East and Southeast Asian cuisines, soy sauce is super versatile and will bring a salty tang to any dish. Unless specified, I always use reduced-sodium light soy.

Toasted Sesame Oil: Use judiciously at the end of cooking for a nutty, sweet, caramelized finish.

ON THE SPICE RACK

I'll be honest, I'm a spice hoarder—but these are the ones I turn to most.

Chili Flakes: A teaspoon will add a gentle kick to pastas, vegetables, eggs—anything!

Ground Cardamom: Gently peppery with a hint of citrus. Often used in tandem with ground cumin and ground coriander.

Ground Coriander: Floral and citrusy—coriander is bright and mildly lemony—it's perfect in both savory and sweet recipes.

Ground Cumin: Earthy, warming, nutty. I use cumin regularly in dressings for depth of flavor, as well as with roasted vegetables and marinades.

Fennel Seeds: Sweet with a mild anise overtone—perfect for seafood and pork.

Five-Spice Powder: This combination of cinnamon, star anise, cloves, fennel, and Szechuan peppercorns is my be-all and end-all. I've grown up with five-spice and use it in everything, both savory and sweet. Think of it as pumpkin spice's sassier sister. Try it in my Mom's Five-Spice Chicken (But on a Sheet Pan) (page 146).

Furikake: This savory Japanese mix finishes any dish to perfection.

Mustard Powder: A quick shortcut to add the mild heat and tang of mustard without adding moisture.

Togarashi: This Japanese spice blend brings heat, sweet and smoky, to any dish.

This _and_ That

Growing up, I was apparently a latchkey kid. (I never really identified with that term—I just felt independent!) While my parents were both in San Francisco working at their architecture firm, I'd leave Old Mill School and make my way home up the winding hills of Mill Valley, with my JanSport backpack securely on my back, hoping that I'd run into a neighbor driving up who could give me a lift (always the best feeling). Once home, I'd fling open some windows for some fresh air, look through the mail for my _Dynamite_ or _MAD_ magazine, put the rice on, and then look for snacks. Armed with my nibbles, and chores done, I'd head to the TV room to catch _Scooby-Doo_. Those few hours alone at home were a bona fide vacation for me—sitting in the cool stillness of the den with the glow of the Zenith TV on my face, I'd happily sip on a bowl of Campbell's soup or ramen, or eat a few slabs of cool watermelon, reveling in the calm before my parents got home. These days, not too much has changed. I'm a fan of a frittata for dinner. Similarly, I'm known to gulp down a bowl of soup at 9 a.m. Why limit yourself? This chapter features recipes that run the gamut from soups (like my Yellow Tomato Soup with Creamy Chili Crisp, page 32) to sandwiches (Hong Kong French Toast Grilled Cheese, page 17) to breakfasty items (Miso Butter Scrams on Toast, page 9) and more. They are meant to be eaten anytime you want, (almost) anywhere you please, solo or with your crew. _Scooby-Doo_ viewing not required.

OEUFS KEWPIE

SERVES 4 TO 6

Here's my twist on the French bistro classic oeufs mayonnaise, a surprisingly simple dish that traditionally is boiled eggs with a dollop of mayonnaise on top. Think of it as deviled eggs but easy, and just as delicious. I love the version at Libertine—one of my favorite West Village restaurants—but here, I've used flavor-packed Japanese Kewpie mayonnaise, which is unctuous, creamy, and instantly saucy, along with scallions, furikake, and, just like at Libertine's, a dollop of salmon roe (optional, but their briny pop will dance against the luxurious sauce on your tongue). Definitely serve with baguette slices.

6 large eggs

KEWPIE SAUCE

2 teaspoons fresh lemon juice

1 tablespoon rice wine vinegar

1 teaspoon white miso

½ cup Kewpie mayonnaise

1 tablespoon Dijon mustard

Kosher salt

Freshly ground black pepper

EVERYTHING ELSE

1 scallion, green part only, thinly sliced

1 tablespoon minced flat-leaf parsley, plus parsley leaves for garnish

1 teaspoon furikake

Salmon roe (optional)

Crusty baguette, sliced, for serving

Bring a medium saucepan of water to a gentle boil. Lower the eggs into the boiling water and cook for 9 minutes. Remove the eggs and immediately plunge into a bowl of ice water to cool completely.

Meanwhile, make the Kewpie sauce. In a small bowl, whisk together the lemon juice, vinegar, and miso until the miso is fully dissolved. Add the mayonnaise, Dijon, a pinch of salt, and ¼ teaspoon pepper and whisk until smooth.

Peel the eggs and halve them, then place cut side down on a flat platter or plate. Drape each egg with some of the sauce, allowing the excess to pool on the platter. Garnish with the scallion, minced parsley, and furikake. Add a small spoonful of salmon roe atop each egg, if you like, then garnish with more parsley. Serve with baguette slices.

2

POTSTICKER FRITTATA

If I have any life advice to give, it's to always have a bag of potstickers in the freezer. From childhood until now, this has been the case for me. I can go to bed at night feeling OK about my life knowing they're there. Give in and let them be there for you too, waiting to be coaxed into steaming juicy tenderness in a piping-hot pan. Adding eggs to the pan near the end of the cooking process yields the best of both worlds—succulent potstickers sitting amid a tender lake of eggs, all with a golden-brown bottom—turning this snack into a main course that's perfect for lunch or brunch or truly anytime.

4 or 5 large eggs

2 scallions, thinly sliced, divided

Kosher salt

Freshly ground black pepper

2 tablespoons neutral oil

8 frozen potstickers

Mixed soft herbs, such as basil, mint, chives, and/or cilantro, for garnish (optional)

Furikake, for finishing

Soy sauce, for serving

Chili oil, for serving (optional)

Whisk the eggs in a small bowl, then stir in half the scallions, ½ teaspoon salt, and ¼ teaspoon pepper.

In a large nonstick skillet, heat the oil over medium-high heat and swirl to coat. Arrange the potstickers in a sunburst formation around the pan, ensuring that they are evenly spaced and sit firmly on their bottom flat side. Let cook for 1 minute, then pour ½ cup water into the center of the pan (leaving the potstickers undisturbed) and cover. Turn the heat down to medium and let them steam for 4 minutes (there will still be some water in the pan). Carefully lift the lid and pour the beaten eggs into the pan, ensuring you don't pour them on top of the dumplings. Cover and continue to cook for 4 to 5 minutes, or until the eggs are set and start to pull away from the sides of the pan, the bottom is golden brown, and the dumplings are cooked through.

Garnish with remaining scallions and herbs (if using), finish with a sprinkle of furikake, and serve right from the pan with soy sauce and chili oil (if using) alongside. Alternatively, you can carefully slide onto a plate to serve.

Hot Tip Top with anything you like—sliced avocado, baby kale, diced ham, and so much more.

Crispy
DEVILED TEA EGGS

MAKES
12 DEVILED
EGGS

The wonderful world of deviled eggs is a treasure trove, and I've given them my own twist. Chinese tea eggs are hard-boiled eggs soaked in a tea-based marinade with a deliciously salty spiced flavor. They're traditionally eaten during the Lunar New Year, but listen, there's no need to eat them only on special occasions. The deviled part here—the yolk—is flavored with oyster sauce and nori and finished with the crunch of panko. These are one-biters in my book.

MARINATED EGGS

2 tablespoons light soy sauce

2 tablespoons dark soy sauce

1 teaspoon Sichuan peppercorns

1 star anise

2 teaspoons sugar

3 black tea bags

6 large eggs

PANKO TOPPING

1 tablespoon extra-virgin olive oil

⅓ cup panko

⅛ teaspoon smoked paprika

¼ cup mix of finely chopped dill and cilantro

Kosher salt

Freshly ground black pepper

EVERYTHING ELSE

3 tablespoons Kewpie mayonnaise

½ teaspoon oyster sauce

½ teaspoon mustard powder

Kosher salt

Freshly ground black pepper

1 sheet nori, finely chopped

1 tablespoon bonito flakes

Dill and cilantro, for garnish

In a small pot, combine the light soy, dark soy, Sichuan peppercorns, star anise, sugar, tea bags, and 1½ cups water. Bring to a boil over medium heat, then turn the heat down, cover, and simmer for 15 minutes. Remove from the heat and let cool completely, then remove and discard the tea bags. Transfer the marinade to an airtight container.

Rinse the pot, fill with fresh water, and bring to a boil. Gently lower the eggs into the boiling water and cook for 9 minutes. Transfer the eggs to a bowl of ice water to cool completely. Peel the eggs and add them to the marinade. Cover and refrigerate for 30 hours, stirring the eggs a few times to ensure the marinade coats all the eggs thoroughly.

To make the panko topping, heat the olive oil in a medium skillet over medium heat until shimmering. Add the panko and smoked paprika and toast, stirring frequently, until golden brown, about 5 minutes. Stir in the herbs, season with salt and pepper, then transfer to a plate and spread out to let cool.

To assemble, remove the eggs from the marinade and cut them in half, wiping the blade clean between each cut. Remove the yolks with a spoon and transfer to a small bowl. Add the mayonnaise, oyster sauce, and mustard powder and whisk until smooth. Season with salt and pepper. Use two spoons to spoon the yolk mixture back into the egg whites.

To serve, spread half the toasted panko on a serving plate, then top with the deviled eggs. Sprinkle with the remaining panko and top with the nori and bonito flakes. Garnish with dill and cilantro and serve.

Try With Serve alongside Sweet and Sour Sticky Ribs with Citrus Peanut Gremolata (page 182).

Remix! For a quick take, simply cut the eggs in half and top with a small dollop of Kewpie mayo.

MISO BUTTER
SCRAMS *on Toast*

SERVES 1 TO 2

All right, let's talk toast because, face it, everything is just better on toast, and scrambled eggs are no exception. But hold up, let me introduce you to these next-level scrams. The real sorcery here? Miso butter. This stuff is the secret flavor bomb that infuses every bite with crazy depth and complexity. The swicy sauce is a marriage of sweet and spicy that takes these eggs to the next level. And to top it all off, a shower of everything bagel seasoning. A perfect snack for whenever that feels a touch jazzy but is so simple to make.

SWICY SAUCE

1 tablespoon gochujang

1 tablespoon ketchup

2 teaspoons Kewpie mayonnaise

1 teaspoon honey

EVERYTHING ELSE

1 tablespoon yellow miso

2 tablespoons unsalted butter, softened

4 large eggs

Kosher salt

Freshly ground black pepper

2 slices good sandwich bread, like pullman, potato, or pain de mie, toasted

Everything bagel seasoning, for finishing

Cilantro, for garnish

To make the swicy sauce, in a small bowl, combine the gochujang, ketchup, mayonnaise, and honey and mix well. Set aside.

In another small bowl, combine the miso and butter and use a fork to thoroughly mix. The more completely combined, the better—so really get in there and mash 'em together. Put half the miso butter in the freezer.

In a medium nonstick skillet, melt the remaining miso butter over low heat. Crack the eggs into the pan and use a spatula to break the yolks and swirl them into the whites. Gently cook the eggs, using your spatula to pull the eggs away from the edge and swirl to create curds, about 4 minutes. Add the reserved cold miso butter, ½ teaspoon salt, and ¼ teaspoon pepper and stir for about 30 seconds. When the eggs are just set, turn them out onto a serving dish.

Spread the swicy sauce onto the toast, then top with the scrams. Finish with everything bagel seasoning, garnish with cilantro, and serve immediately.

Try With Swicy sauce is not just for eggs. It will give a kick to Quick Scallion Pancakes (page 18), or you can slather it on salmon, burgers, roasted veggies, or pork chops.

SHAKSHUKA
EGG *in the* HOLE

SERVES 4

Talk about a one-dish meal that will most definitely feed a crowd! I've given traditional shakshuka a spin—adding Shaoxing rice wine, soy sauce, and fish sauce to the tomatoes for a long-simmered taste—and topped everything off with bread. And yep, that's where the hole comes in—crack that egg in the hole, bake it off until set, and serve. Bright tomato sauce-y goodness and crunchy toasted bread nestling a sunny-side up egg. Hello, gorgeous.

4 large ½- to ¾-inch slices sourdough or country bread (from a boule)

2 tablespoons unsalted butter, softened

2 tablespoons extra-virgin olive oil

2 teaspoons smoked paprika

1 teaspoon ground cumin

1 teaspoon chili powder

1 medium red onion, thinly sliced

1 red bell pepper, cored, seeded, and thinly sliced

3 garlic cloves, thinly sliced

1 tablespoon Shaoxing rice wine

1 tablespoon soy sauce

1 tablespoon Vietnamese fish sauce

1 (28-ounce) can whole peeled tomatoes

¼ cup roughly chopped cilantro, plus more for garnish

¼ cup roughly chopped flat-leaf parsley, plus more for garnish

Kosher salt

Freshly ground black pepper

4 large eggs

Chili crisp, for serving

Preheat the oven to 400°F with a rack in the middle position.

Using a 2¼-inch biscuit cutter, cut a hole out of the center of each slice of bread. Spread one side of each slice with butter and set aside.

Heat the olive oil in a 12-inch cast-iron or other ovenproof skillet (the pan needs to be large enough to fit the bread slices in a single layer) over medium heat. Add the paprika, cumin, and chili powder, then the onion, bell pepper, and garlic, and cook until starting to soften, about 5 minutes. Add the rice wine, soy sauce, and fish sauce and let reduce for 1 minute. Add the tomatoes and their juice, crushing the tomatoes with your hands as you add them, along with the cilantro and parsley, and use a spoon to break them down a bit. Season with salt and pepper. Turn the heat down and simmer for 7 to 8 minutes, or until the sauce has reduced and thickened a bit.

Place the prepared bread on top of the tomato mixture and carefully crack an egg into each hole (you can also crack each egg into a small bowl first, then pour it into the hole). Place the skillet in the oven and bake for 8 minutes, or until the eggs are set and the bread is golden brown.

Garnish with additional cilantro and parsley and serve warm, with chili crisp alongside.

Hot Tip If you don't have a biscuit cutter, use the rim of a drinking glass or a metal measuring cup.

Remix! Feel free to toss in a handful of feta atop the sauce just before laying down the bread.

CHINESE STEAMED EGG *with Parm, Bacon, and Sourdough*

SERVES 2

Let's dive into the nostalgic world of Chinese steamed egg. Jing seui daan, which translates to "steamed water egg" in Cantonese, is a dish that should practically be a family heirloom—Mom has regularly made it for decades using Grandma's recipe. In the traditional Cantonese homestyle dish, water and egg join forces and are whipped until velvety smooth, then steamed into jiggly, supple perfection and topped with a variety of condiments, such as salted fish or pork floss. Here, I've taken a page from my breakfasts growing up and have added bacon for that meaty, salty bite and sourdough for crunch, and finished everything off with a shower of freshly grated Parmigiano-Reggiano.

3 large eggs

½ cup freshly grated parmesan cheese, divided

1½ cups low-sodium chicken stock

Kosher salt

Freshly ground black pepper

3 bacon strips

1 cup torn sourdough bread (small bite-size pieces)

1½ teaspoons furikake

1 tablespoon minced chives

1½ teaspoons maple syrup

Soy sauce, for serving

In a medium bowl, whisk together the eggs and ¼ cup of the parmesan, then add the chicken stock, ¼ teaspoon salt, and a pinch of pepper and whisk until smooth, at least 30 seconds. Pour into an 8- to 9-inch-diameter shallow heatproof bowl or pie plate and skim any bubbles from the surface. Cover with plastic wrap or a plate.

Bring 1 inch water to a boil in a deep skillet or a wide pot fitted with a steam rack (the pan should be slightly larger than the bowl). Carefully lower the bowl onto the rack, turn the heat down to medium-low, cover, and steam for 15 minutes, or until the eggs are set but still wobbly.

Meanwhile, cook the bacon in a large skillet over medium heat to the desired crispness, then transfer to a paper towel–lined plate. Cool and cut into large dice. Add the sourdough bread to the bacon grease left in the pan and toast until golden brown, 2 to 3 minutes. Transfer to the same paper towel–lined plate.

Sprinkle the remaining ¼ cup parmesan and the furikake on the eggs, then top with the sourdough and bacon. Garnish with the chives, drizzle with the maple syrup, and serve immediately, with soy sauce alongside.

Remix! This dish is super versatile when it comes to toppings, so get creative! Swap in kimchi, bonito flakes, or cooked lap cheong. Or, for a truly Zen experience, eat it without toppings and just a dash of soy sauce.

Burnt Miso
CINNAMON TOAST

SERVES 2

A childhood favorite revisited, but with the deep flavor of brown sugar and a hit of miso. The caramelized crunch and chew of the crust against the pillowy interior of the bread is a dreamy snack situation.

2 tablespoons salted butter, softened

2 tablespoons dark brown sugar

2 teaspoons miso

1 teaspoon ground cinnamon

½ teaspoon five-spice powder

2 thick slices milk bread or brioche

Combine the butter, brown sugar, miso, cinnamon, and five-spice in a bowl and mix well.

Spread half the butter mixture on one side of the bread slices, then place buttered side down in a large nonstick skillet over medium-low heat. Spread the remaining mixture on the second sides. Cook for 2 to 2½ minutes, or until dark brown on the bottom, then flip and cook for another minute. It will look almost burnt; don't worry, but do watch it carefully so it doesn't actually burn. Transfer to a wire rack (or a few chopsticks set 2 inches apart) to cool for 1 to 2 minutes, then serve.

Hot Tip Thick slices, in this case, means 1 to even 2 inches thick.

Remix! Make it into a sandwich! Fill with Nutella, or make an over-the-top PB&J.

Hong Kong
FRENCH TOAST GRILLED CHEESE

MAKES
2 SANDWICHES

There are certain dishes that are unique to Hong Kong, and Hong Kong French toast is one of them. Born out of the years of British rule, this indulgent situation traditionally is a triple-decker towering beauty of white bread, filled with peanut butter, dipped into egg and fried, and served with a liberal drizzle of golden syrup or condensed milk. Here I've skipped the peanut butter and swapped in cheese for a decidedly more savory—and perhaps even more decadent—take on the classic.

6 slices milk bread or pullman loaf

¼ cup mascarpone

Kosher salt

Freshly ground black pepper

4 slices American cheese

4 slices Monterey Jack cheese

2 large eggs

1 cup panko

Neutral oil, for frying

1 tablespoon unsalted butter

Maple syrup, for serving

Grated lemon zest, for finishing

Flaky sea salt, for finishing

Trim all the bread slices to be the same size, using a slice of American cheese as your guide.

Set 2 slices of bread on a cutting board. Spread each slice with half the mascarpone, then season with kosher salt and pepper. Layer atop each 1 slice of American cheese and 1 slice of Monterey Jack. Layer both sandwiches with a second slice of bread (this will be the middle piece of bread), then spread that middle slice with the remaining mascarpone and season with kosher salt and pepper. And again, layer atop both sandwiches 1 slice of American and 1 slice of Monterey Jack. Top each sandwich with the final 2 slices of bread.

In a shallow bowl, beat the eggs and season with kosher salt and pepper. Put the panko in a second bowl. Carefully coat each sandwich on all sides with egg, then with panko.

In a large skillet, heat a thin layer of neutral oil along with the butter over medium-low heat. Fry the sandwiches, working in batches as needed, until golden brown on all sides and the cheese is melted, 1 to 1½ minutes on each side and 30 to 40 seconds on the edges. Transfer to serving plates.

Drizzle each sandwich with maple syrup, finish with lemon zest and flaky sea salt, and serve immediately.

Hot Tip Any good-quality white bread will work here.

Try With Yellow Tomato Soup with Creamy Chili Crisp (page 32).

Quick
SCALLION PANCAKES

MAKES
6 (9-INCH)
PANCAKES

OK, let me set the record straight: These are not the traditional Chinese kind of scallion pancakes, which are undeniably tasty but have a few steps and techniques that require a bit more patience than I usually have. When I'm in that mood, I turn to these babies. Crunchy exterior, pillowy interior with just a bit of chew (from the rice flour), and packed with scallions, cheddar, kimchi, and Spam. A dunk in a quick soy dipping sauce adds brightness. 'Cause honestly, who needs patience when you've got this level of *yum* at your very fingertips?

1 cup rice flour

1 cup all-purpose flour

2 tablespoons sweet (glutinous) rice flour

1 tablespoon instant yeast

Kosher salt

½ cup kimchi

1 bunch scallions, cut into 2-inch pieces

1 cup shredded cheddar

1 cup ¼-inch cubes Spam

1 small jalapeño, seeded and thinly sliced

Neutral oil, for frying

Toasted sesame seeds, for garnish

DIPPING SAUCE

2 tablespoons soy sauce

2 tablespoons rice wine vinegar

1 teaspoon honey

In a large bowl, combine the rice flour, all-purpose flour, glutinous rice flour, yeast, 1 teaspoon salt, and 3 cups warm water (110°F to 120°F) and whisk until just incorporated and smooth. Cover and let sit for 30 minutes. You'll see some bubbles from the active yeast. Note that the batter will separate, but don't worry.

Meanwhile, make the dipping sauce. In a small bowl, whisk together the soy sauce, rice wine vinegar, and honey; set aside until ready to serve.

Squeeze the kimchi of all its liquid and roughly chop, then add it to the dough. Gently fold it in, along with the scallions, cheddar, Spam, and jalapeño.

Heat a large cast-iron or nonstick skillet over medium heat. Add just enough oil to coat the surface of the pan and fry ½-cup portions of the dough mixture until golden brown, about 3 minutes per side.

Sprinkle with sesame seeds, then serve hot with the dipping sauce.

Try With Add swicy sauce (page 9) as a second sauce option for some sweet heat.

Remix! You can use ham instead of Spam or omit the meat completely.

BAKED CAMEMBERT
with Chili Crisp and Honey

SERVES 4 TO 6

There always seemed to be a wheel of Camembert in the fridge when I was a kid. For Mom, forever enchanted by the allure of French cuisine, a slice of Camembert was the quickest shortcut to transport her back to our family trips to France. We would jam into our small rental car with a paper sack cradling a fresh baguette, a wheel of Camembert, perhaps some thinly sliced jambon de Paris, and an orange or two. Our impromptu feast unfolded on the side of a country road, using the car trunk as our makeshift table. Here is my take on the perennial baked party favorite, with flavors that dance between heat, sweet, and citrus.

1 (8-ounce) wheel Camembert

1 tablespoon orange marmalade

1 tablespoon chili crisp

2 teaspoons grated orange zest

Flaky sea salt, for finishing

Toasted country bread or crackers, for serving

Preheat the oven to 350°F.

If your cheese comes in a wooden container, remove the top, unwrap the cheese, and place the cheese back in the container. Place the cheese (in its wooden container or not) in a small ovenproof skillet or baking dish. Spread the marmalade in an even layer atop the cheese. Bake for 10 to 12 minutes, until soft to the touch and fully melted.

Transfer to a serving plate. Drizzle with the chili crisp, sprinkle with the orange zest, and finish with some flaky sea salt. Serve with toasted bread or crackers alongside.

Remix! Instead of Camembert, use Brie or any other wheel of soft, triple-cream type cheese.

Quick PICKLED CUKES

SERVES 6 TO 8

While writing this cookbook, I texted several family members asking for any food memories of Grandma. My sister, Indigo, and cousin Chia-Lien immediately replied with "the pickled cucumbers!" I could not believe that I'd completely forgotten about them. They were always on Grandma's dining table, and for good reason—they're the perfect easy bite to add tangy goodness to a meal, and take no time whatsoever. Here's her recipe.

½ cup apple cider vinegar

½ cup sugar

4 fat garlic cloves, thinly sliced

Kosher salt

4 to 5 mini cucumbers

In a small bowl, combine the vinegar, sugar, garlic, 1 teaspoon salt, and ¼ cup hot water. Stir to dissolve most of the sugar (it will continue to dissolve as it sits).

Thinly slice the cucumbers on a mandoline or with a very sharp knife. Add to the bowl, stir to combine, and let sit for 15 to 30 minutes before serving.

Try With Serve these pickles alongside Caramel Cod with Fragrant Lime Coconut Rice (page 116) or Pork Meatloaf with Salted Egg Yolk (page 179).

Hot Tip These are best eaten the day they are made.

Remix! Add a few dashes of sriracha for a spicy kick.

RADISHES
with Oyster Butter

Dipping radishes into fine butter is *très français*—a classic bistro dish that's quite the elegant nibble. A swipe of butter, a touch of flaky sea salt—how simple and perfect can it get? Here, the butter game gets notched up a few pegs with the savory-sweet tang of oyster sauce, and sesame seeds add another layer of nutty crunch alongside those signature flaky shards of salt.

1 bunch radishes, scrubbed clean and dried well

5 tablespoons unsalted European-style butter, softened

1 teaspoon oyster sauce

1 tablespoon flaky sea salt

½ teaspoon sugar

1 tablespoon black sesame seeds

If your radish tops are pretty, keep them on, otherwise trim them.

In a small bowl, mix the butter with the oyster sauce.

Arrange the radishes on a platter. In a small bowl, mix the flaky sea salt and sugar, then spoon onto the platter in a small pile. Spoon the sesame seeds in a separate pile on the platter.

To eat, dip a radish in the oyster butter (or use a small knife to spread it), then dip in the sesame seeds and finish with a pinch of the flaky sea salt mixture.

Hot Tip While you can buy radishes year-round in the grocery store, it's worth seeking out your gourmet grocery store or farmers' market for in-season heirloom varieties like French Breakfast.

Remix! If you can't find black sesame seeds, use white, but toast them in a dry pan for 1 to 2 minutes to bring out their flavor.

"PRAWN" *and* PROSCIUTTO

SERVES 4 TO 6

Rainbow-hued shrimp chips (also known as prawn crackers) hold serious nostalgia for me. They're featherweight with a delicate crunch and were ubiquitous at every Chinese banquet when I was growing up, usually as a garnish dotting the rim of a platter heaving with roast duck or squab. Inspired by the chip and Iberico ham tower at Ernesto's in NYC, I've given shrimp chips the starring treatment here—piled high on a plate with prosciutto, they're the ideal party app or fun nibble-friendly starter.

4 ounces very thinly sliced prosciutto, torn into strips

2½ to 3 ounces fried multicolored shrimp chips

1 teaspoon light brown sugar

Grated zest of 1 small lemon

Togarashi, for finishing

Lay down a few strips of prosciutto on a large plate (this will help the chips from sliding), then pile the shrimp chips and prosciutto on the plate, ensuring that the prosciutto is layered throughout. Sprinkle with the brown sugar, then zest the lemon directly atop. Finish with togarashi and serve.

Hot Tip You can find shrimp chips at many Asian markets, either already fried or uncooked, in which case follow the package directions to fry them up. Don't worry if you can't find the multicolored ones, as any shrimp or prawn cracker will work.

CARROT GOCHUJANG HUMMUS

MAKES 6 CUPS

Carrots hold an undisputable rank in my personal vegetable hall of fame (for sure they're in my top 3). Introducing them—roasted—to hummus brings forth a beautiful caramelized sweetness that plays so well with the earthy kick of gochujang and the mellow nuttiness of tahini. I love serving this hummus with multicolored carrots for a serious carrot-on-carrot experience, but any crudités, cracker, or bread will do just fine.

1½ pounds carrots (about 2 bunches), cut into 1-inch rounds

4 tablespoons extra-virgin olive oil, divided, plus more for serving

Kosher salt

Freshly ground black pepper

1 (15-ounce) can chickpeas, drained and rinsed

½ cup tahini

2 tablespoons gochujang

1 tablespoon yellow miso

2 teaspoons toasted sesame oil

½ teaspoon five-spice powder, plus more for serving

Toasted sesame seeds, for garnish

1 scallion, thinly sliced, for garnish

Crudités and country bread, for serving

Preheat the oven to 425°F. Line a rimmed baking sheet with parchment paper.

Put the carrots on the prepared baking sheet, toss with 1 tablespoon of the olive oil, and season with a pinch of salt and pepper. Roast for 30 to 35 minutes, or until the carrots are browned in spots and very tender when pierced with a knife. Remove from the oven and let cool.

Transfer the carrots to a blender and add the remaining 3 tablespoons olive oil, chickpeas, tahini, gochujang, miso, sesame oil, five-spice, and ½ cup ice-cold water. Puree until smooth, adding more water, 1 table-spoon at a time, to thin out the hummus to the desired consistency—the mixture should be very smooth and creamy. Season with salt and pepper.

Transfer to a bowl and use a spoon to swirl. Drizzle with additional olive oil, finish with a pinch of five-spice, and garnish with sesame seeds and scallion. Serve with crudités and bread.

Granny Ong's
CHICKEN ESSENCE

SERVES 2

Granny Ong—my dad's stepmother—would make gai jing (which literally translates to "chicken essence") for my sister and me every time we visited her in Phoenix. There, at the plastic-covered dining table with a view to her hearty garden visible through the sliding glass doors, she'd serve us large steaming bowls of the magical elixir, all the while scurrying to and fro in the kitchen behind us, speaking Cantonese at a breakneck speed (to this day, I can still only catch maybe every third word). We'd dutifully sip away, feeling every ache or sniffle magically disappear. Chinese penicillin, this is.

And listen, calling this dish a soup or even a broth doesn't seem right—it's truly the deepest and most fundamental quintessence of chicken. Unlike a broth or stock, where the chicken parts are submerged in water along with other aromatics, here the bird meets only steam. That steam cooks the bird, and whatever liquid that is cooked off is captured, strained, and served. A Granny Ong–approved cure-all, embodying the pure elemental flavor of chicken, this is a true tonic for body and soul.

1 (2- to 3-pound) chicken
Kosher salt
Pinch ground white pepper

On a clean cutting board, pat the chicken dry with a paper towel and break it down into pieces using a very sharp knife or cleaver. Separate each thigh and drumstick, separate the wings and drumettes, and cut the breasts into halves or thirds. Cut down the remaining carcass as best you can (there is no exact science here).

Cover the chicken pieces with plastic wrap and use a mallet or a heavy skillet or pot to gently pound each piece so it's slightly flattened.

Place a small heatproof bowl upside-down inside a large heatproof bowl. Arrange the chicken pieces around and atop the dome of the smaller bowl (if your chicken is piled over the rim of the large bowl, get a larger bowl). Cover the large bowl with a heatproof plate or wrap it tightly with aluminum foil. The smaller bowl will serve as a reservoir to catch the essence. Carefully place the bowl in a large stockpot. Add water to the pot to come halfway up the bowl.

Cover the pot and bring the water to a boil, then turn the heat down and simmer, covered, for 4 hours. Check periodically to ensure that there's still enough water in the pot. *(recipe continues)*

Turn off the heat. Carefully remove the large bowl from the pot, uncover it, and remove the chicken and then the small bowl. Strain the essence remaining in the pot through a fine-mesh sieve into a clean bowl. Season lightly with salt and a pinch of white pepper, then pour into bowls and serve hot. If you like, you may shred the chicken and add it to the essence before serving.

Hot Tip Use the best-quality bird you can find 'cause besides salt and pepper, it's the only ingredient. Look for an organic, free-range chicken.

Try With While it's usually served unadorned, feel free to add sliced ginger, a chopped scallion, a few cilantro sprigs, or some goji berries atop the chicken before steaming. But go easy, as you don't want anything to overpower the pure chicken flavor.

Granny Ong and Grandma Mary deciding which piece of fish is best.

PARM WONTON BROTH

SERVES 6 TO 8

In my freezer, there's always a stash of saved parmesan rinds (you can also buy them at many grocery stores, where they're already packaged up and ready to use). They are perfect for amping up flavor in soups or stews, but there's something truly enchanting about the unadulterated flavor of pure Italian parmesan broth—brodo di parmigiano—that echoes miso broth in its simplicity but results in its own uniquely complex and nuanced flavor. It's very much a Zen-like canvas, patiently waiting for the starring roles of wontons and tofu.

3 tablespoons extra-virgin olive oil

3 medium shallots, unpeeled, root ends trimmed, and halved

1 medium yellow onion, quartered

1 small head garlic, halved crosswise

½ cup dry white wine

1 pound parmesan rinds

1 teaspoon whole black peppercorns

12 flat-leaf parsley sprigs

12 cilantro sprigs

Kosher salt

2 tablespoons Vietnamese fish sauce, plus more for serving (optional)

8 ounces button mushrooms, sliced

8 ounces frozen wontons or dumplings

7 to 8 ounces firm tofu, cut into ½-inch cubes

2 cups baby spinach (about 2 ounces)

½ cup frozen peas

Freshly ground black pepper

Chili crisp, for serving

In a medium stockpot or Dutch oven, heat the olive oil over medium heat. Add the shallots and onion cut side down and cook until golden brown, about 3 minutes, then add the garlic cut side down. Stir and continue to cook for 1 to 2 minutes, until the garlic is browned in spots.

Add the white wine, stir, and cook for 30 seconds, then add the parmesan rinds, peppercorns, parsley, and cilantro. Season with a pinch of kosher salt, then add 12 cups water and the fish sauce. Bring to a boil, then partially cover the pot and simmer, stirring occasionally, for 2 hours, or until the broth is reduced by half, is dark in color, and is flavorful and intensely parm-y. Strain the broth through a fine-mesh sieve (or a colander lined with cheesecloth) into a large bowl or pot. Discard the solids.

Clean the pot and return the stock to it. Bring to a gentle boil, then turn the heat down to medium and add the mushrooms, wontons, and tofu. Simmer for 6 to 8 minutes, or until the wontons are cooked. Stir in the spinach and peas. Season with salt and pepper.

To serve, pour into bowls and finish with a small glug of fish sauce, if you like, and a small dollop of chili crisp.

Hot Tip Make the broth a day in advance and refrigerate overnight to allow the flavors to meld.

Try With Parmesan broth is a super versatile base for any kind of soup. Try it with the turkey meatballs from my Turkey Meatballs with Corn, Stone Fruit, and Sumac Labneh (page 158).

Remix! Replace the spinach with kale, escarole, or any other hearty leafy green.

YELLOW TOMATO SOUP
with Creamy Chili Crisp

SERVES 4

Tomato soup was a mainstay in our home growing up—and I mean specifically of the Campbell's variety. To be honest, the thought of making it from scratch never even crossed our minds. Opening a can, heating it in a saucepan, and slurping it with some saltines on the side was my ideal snack growing up. It wasn't until I graduated college and moved to New York that the idea of making it even dawned on me. Well, many years later and with many pots of homemade tomato soup under my belt, here's a special take using yellow cherry tomatoes, which have a lower acidity and a mild sweetness to them. Fish sauce (trust me) adds a nuanced depth of flavor.

4 pounds yellow cherry tomatoes

5 medium shallots, trimmed and quartered

5 garlic cloves, peeled and lightly smashed

Kosher salt

Freshly ground black pepper

¼ cup extra-virgin olive oil, plus more for finishing

3 or 4 thyme sprigs

½ teaspoon ground turmeric

2 teaspoons Vietnamese fish sauce

½ to 1½ cups low-sodium vegetable broth

¼ cup heavy cream

CROUTONS

8 ounces sourdough bread, torn into bite-size pieces

2 tablespoons extra-virgin olive oil

CREAMY CHILI CRISP

¼ cup sour cream

1 tablespoon chili crisp

Preheat the oven to 425°F with racks in the upper and lower thirds of the oven.

Divide the cherry tomatoes, shallots, and garlic between two rimmed baking sheets. Season with 2 teaspoons salt and 1 teaspoon pepper, then add the olive oil and toss to coat. Tuck the thyme sprigs under the tomatoes (so they don't burn in the oven) and sprinkle with the turmeric. Roast for 35 to 40 minutes, swapping the pans halfway through, or until the tomatoes are burst and slightly charred. Remove the thyme sprigs, then let the tomatoes cool for 10 minutes. Leave the oven on.

To make the croutons, toss the sourdough pieces on another rimmed baking sheet with the olive oil, then spread out in a single layer. Toast in the oven for 10 to 15 minutes, or until golden brown.

Transfer the tomatoes and garlic, along with any pan juices, to a stockpot. Add the fish sauce, ½ cup broth, and heavy cream, then use an immersion blender to puree until smooth. Add more broth as needed to achieve the desired consistency. (Alternatively, combine everything in a countertop blender, working in batches, and puree until smooth.)

To make the creamy chili crisp, combine the sour cream and chili crisp in a small bowl and stir together until just combined (a few streaks of chili crisp are great).

To serve, ladle the soup into bowls, finish with a swirl of creamy chili crisp, add a glug of extra-virgin olive oil, and top with the croutons.

Try With Ditch the croutons and serve with Hong Kong French Toast Grilled Cheese (page 17).

Remix! Use red cherry tomatoes if yellow aren't available.

Matzo Ball
EGG DROP SOUP

SERVES 4 TO 6 Why not double your comfort? While Grandma, who made egg drop soup regularly, would probably raise her eyebrows at this combination, for me it hits all the points for what I want a soup to be: fluffy, tender matzo balls (with just a hint of five-spice powder) floating serenely in a savory full-bodied broth with swirls of golden egg. A perfect way to stave off a cold winter's day.

MATZO BALLS

3 large eggs

3 tablespoons neutral oil

¾ cup matzo meal

1 teaspoon baking powder

½ teaspoon five-spice powder

Kosher salt

Freshly ground black pepper

3 tablespoons seltzer, at room temperature

SOUP

6 cups chicken stock

1 teaspoon toasted sesame oil

1 teaspoon ground turmeric

1 teaspoon ground white pepper

Kosher salt

2 tablespoons cornstarch

3 large eggs

1 bunch scallions, thinly sliced, divided

Dill fronds, for garnish

To make the matzo balls, in a medium bowl, combine the eggs and neutral oil and whisk with a fork until combined. Add the matzo meal, baking powder, five-spice powder, 1 teaspoon salt, and ½ teaspoon pepper and use the fork to combine. Add the seltzer and mix until just combined; do not overmix. Cover the bowl and refrigerate for at least 30 minutes or up to overnight. Once chilled, use an ice cream scoop (or your hands) to form into 12 equal balls.

To make the soup, in a Dutch oven or stockpot, combine the chicken stock and 2 cups water, along with the sesame oil, turmeric, white pepper, and salt. Bring to a boil, then turn the heat down and simmer for 1 to 2 minutes.

Add the matzo balls to the soup and simmer for 50 minutes, or until fluffy and tender.

In a small bowl, mix the cornstarch with ¼ cup water until fully combined, then stream the mixture into the broth, while stirring the broth constantly with a wooden spoon.

In a measuring cup or small pitcher (you'll need a spout to easily pour the eggs), beat the eggs with 2 tablespoons water until fully combined. Stream the eggs into the soup while stirring constantly. Stir in the scallions, leaving a little bit behind for garnish.

Ladle the soup and matzo balls into bowls, garnish with the reserved scallions and dill, and serve immediately.

Have You Eaten Your Vegetables?

The Queen of Vegetables, that's my mom. Every night at dinner, her first query to my sister and me was "Have you had your four servings of fruit and vegetables today?" In truth, Mom was a veg lover way before it was cool. Maybe she was secretly pals with Alice Waters across the bay in her Chez Panisse garden? Not likely. In a time when supermarkets had one kind of lettuce (iceberg, of course) and one kind of tomato (tasteless and pink), Mom would go to lengths to find the best quality and variety possible. Small independent grocery stores, farm stands, and Chinatown markets all were likely places to spot Mom, her critical gaze sweeping the stands for the best long beans or butter lettuce. Even today,

each bok choy is carefully inspected before being dropped into a bag. I, too, love my vegetables—whether raw or roasted or charred or blanched—the crunch, chew, or sweetness they add to a meal is unmatched. Vegetables truly have become the most important part of my dinner.

This chapter is divided into two sections—Salads and Not Salads—and the recipes range from bright and happy, like my Summery Corn with Cilantro Lime Vinaigrette (page 41), to deep and rich and meaty (without the meat), like my Fancy Mushrooms and Creamy Beans with Citrus Brown Butter (page 75). Eat your veggies, Mom would say. Indeed!

ASPARAGUS *and* FENNEL
with Gribiche-y Dressing

SERVES 4

Let's talk asparagus! It's a personal favorite of mine and it's made even more delicious when paired with gribiche, a classic French sauce made from hard-boiled eggs and served with steamed asparagus. I've simplified things by removing the eggs from the dressing and instead adding them to the salad, along with thinly sliced fennel for a bit of crunch. Roasting the asparagus on high heat amplifies their flavor (and lets the oven do all the work lickety-split). The dressing? Still gribiche-like with the tang of capers and cornichons and the creamy kick of Dijon. Perfect for a spring lunch.

2 large eggs

1 medium fennel bulb

1 pound asparagus, trimmed

1 teaspoon extra-virgin olive oil

Kosher salt

Freshly ground black pepper

2 cups baby spinach

1 avocado, peeled, pitted, and sliced

Furikake, for garnish

GRIBICHE VINAIGRETTE

Juice of 1 lemon (about 2 tablespoons)

1 teaspoon Dijon mustard

1 teaspoon whole-grain mustard

½ teaspoon maple syrup

¼ cup extra-virgin olive oil

¼ cup cornichons, finely chopped

2 tablespoons capers, drained and rinsed

Kosher salt

Freshly ground black pepper

Place an oven rack 4 inches from the heat source and set the oven to broil.

Bring a small saucepan of water to a boil over high heat, then reduce the heat to medium for a gentle boil. Lower the eggs into the saucepan and simmer for 7 minutes. Transfer to a bowl of ice water to cool, then peel and cut lengthwise into quarters.

Halve and core the fennel (reserve the fronds for garnish), then use a mandoline or very sharp knife to cut into very thin slices.

Spread out the asparagus in a single layer on a rimmed baking sheet, drizzle with the olive oil, and season with salt and pepper. Broil for 2 to 3 minutes, then toss the asparagus and continue to broil for 2 to 3 minutes more, or until the asparagus are charred in spots and tender.

To make the vinaigrette, combine the lemon juice, Dijon, whole-grain mustard, and maple syrup in a small bowl, then whisk in the olive oil. Stir in the cornichons and capers, then season with salt and pepper.

To serve, put the fennel and spinach on a serving platter, add some of the vinaigrette, and gently toss to combine. Arrange the asparagus atop, along with the avocado, then the eggs. Drizzle with more vinaigrette, finish with a pinch of furikake, garnish with the reserved fennel fronds, and serve.

Hot Tip The vinaigrette and eggs can be made a day ahead of time and stored overnight in the refrigerator.

Try With Panko Salmon with Labneh Dijonnaise (page 123).

SUMMERY CORN
with Cilantro Lime Vinaigrette

SERVES 4 When the corn arrives in August, I know that peak summer has arrived. This salad truly is my warm-weather dream dish: full of tender kernels, lots of herbs, and a bright, peppy vinaigrette. And best of all, it comes together in no time at all.

5 ears corn, shucked

3 limes, halved

1 (15-ounce) can chickpeas, drained and rinsed

1 pint cherry tomatoes, halved

Kosher salt

Freshly ground black pepper

¼ cup torn basil leaves, for garnish

¼ cup cilantro leaves, for garnish

2 tablespoons roughly chopped dill fronds, for garnish

CILANTRO LIME VINAIGRETTE

1½ cups packed cilantro leaves and tender stems

⅓ cup extra-virgin olive oil

1 tablespoon Vietnamese fish sauce

1 tablespoon maple syrup

¼ teaspoon smoked paprika

¼ teaspoon ground sumac

Kosher salt

Freshly ground black pepper

Heat a grill to high heat.

Place the ears of corn on the grill, along with the lime halves, cut side down. Remove the limes after about 3 minutes, or when the flesh has grill marks, and set aside for the vinaigrette. Cook the corn, rotating occasionally, until the kernels are tender and charred in spots, about 10 minutes total. Remove from the grill and let cool.

To make the vinaigrette, juice the grilled limes. Transfer ⅓ cup of the grilled lime juice to a food processor or blender and add the cilantro, olive oil, fish sauce, maple syrup, paprika, and sumac. Blend until smooth, then season with ½ teaspoon salt and ¼ teaspoon pepper.

Cut the corn kernels off the cobs and transfer to a serving bowl. Add the chickpeas and cherry tomatoes, then season with ½ teaspoon salt and ¼ teaspoon pepper and toss. Add the vinaigrette and mix to combine. Garnish with the basil, cilantro, and dill and serve.

Try With Char Siu Bacon Cheeseburger (page 170).

Mix In Use any mix of soft herbs you like—mint, flat-leaf parsley, and tarragon are all great in this salad.

Hot Tip No grill? No problem. You can cut the corn kernels off the cobs and sauté in a pan over medium heat until just tender and charred in spots, about 10 minutes.

Remix! Add 8 ounces bocconcini or shavings of Pecorino Romano if you like.

HONEYDEW *and* CUCUMBER *with Halloumi and Togarashi Hot Honey*

This fresh, versatile salad comes together in a flash. I love using halloumi—it lends heft to this dish, and that squeaky-tender bounce as you take a bite? Pure satisfaction.

TOGARASHI HOT HONEY

¼ cup honey

1 tablespoon chili flakes

1½ teaspoons apple cider vinegar

1 to 2 teaspoons togarashi

EVERYTHING ELSE

1 small honeydew melon

2 mini cucumbers

1 pound halloumi, sliced into ½-inch planks

2 tablespoons extra-virgin olive oil, divided

1 tablespoon rice wine vinegar

¼ cup mint leaves

¼ cup basil leaves

1 sheet nori, chopped or crushed into small pieces

Flaky sea salt

To make the hot honey, combine the honey and chili flakes in a small saucepan and simmer over medium-low heat just until the honey is softened, about 1 minute. Remove the pan from the heat and let sit for 5 minutes, then pour the honey through a fine-mesh sieve into a small bowl. Stir in the apple cider vinegar and togarashi and let cool completely.

Peel the honeydew, scoop out the seeds, and slice into very thin slices (use a mandoline or a very sharp knife). Trim the cucumbers and use a mandoline to cut into very thin rounds.

Rub the halloumi on both sides with 1 tablespoon of the olive oil and, working in batches as necessary, grill on a stovetop grill over medium heat for 2 to 3 minutes per side, or until golden brown.

To assemble, arrange the halloumi, honeydew, and cucumbers on a serving platter. Drizzle with the rice wine vinegar and remaining 1 tablespoon olive oil, followed by the hot honey. Garnish with the mint and basil, then finish with the nori and flaky sea salt and serve.

Hot Tip Drizzle the hot honey on fried chicken or over roasted vegetables, or add it to a stir-fry.

Try With Summer Roll Fish Tacos with Spicy Peanut Sauce (page 135).

Remix! Instead of honeydew, try watermelon, cantaloupe, or mango. If you can't find togarashi, use furikake or a mix of cayenne pepper and toasted sesame seeds.

Super Fresh
SNAP PEA SALAD

SERVES 4

When these beauties are in season, the less you do with them the better. This salad keeps it super easy, as you don't even have to blanch the sugar snaps—they're thinly sliced and tossed with pistachios for more crunch, Pecorino Romano for a salty, savory kick, and lots of fresh herbs. A simple vinaigrette brings it all together! Easy-peasy, and you're eating in about 15 minutes.

3 tablespoons extra-virgin olive oil

2 tablespoons fresh lemon juice

1 tablespoon rice wine vinegar

2 teaspoons honey

Pinch chili flakes (optional)

Kosher salt

Freshly ground black pepper

1 pound sugar snap peas, trimmed and thinly sliced lengthwise

⅓ cup freshly grated Pecorino Romano

¼ cup roughly chopped pistachios

2 tablespoons minced chives

2 tablespoons mint leaves

In a large serving bowl, whisk together the olive oil, lemon juice, rice wine vinegar, honey, and chili flakes (if using). Season with 1 teaspoon salt and ¼ teaspoon pepper and whisk until emulsified.

Add the sugar snap peas to the bowl and toss to coat. Sprinkle an even layer of Pecorino Romano atop, garnish with the pistachios, then finish with the chives and mint.

Try With Sweet and Sour Spicy Tofu and Chickpeas (page 194).

Remix! No sugar snaps? No problem. This salad is also great with 4 cups thawed frozen peas.

RADICCHIO
and FENNEL SALAD
with Creamy Miso Maple Dressing

SERVES 4

While I could very likely eat this salad all year long, my true affection for it blossoms in the colder months, when winter has pulled its gray sheet across the sky, lopping off too many hours to the day. Chicory and citrus are truly winter's bright joys, and I lean hard into them during these moody months, which may be the only explanation as to why I don't get the seasonal blues. That dependable radicchio holds up well to vinaigrette and is the perfect foil for all the other crunchy, savory, creamy things to keep it interesting, 'cause listen, nobody wants a boring salad. If you can find pink radicchio (I get it from Campo Rosso Farm at the Union Square Greenmarket in NYC, so try your local farm stand or gourmet grocery store) or other varieties of chicory such as endive, for sure use them. Add sliced chicken breast atop for a one-dish lunch.

**CREAMY MISO
MAPLE DRESSING**

¼ cup yellow miso

¼ cup rice wine vinegar

1 tablespoon fresh lemon juice

¼ cup extra-virgin olive oil

2½ tablespoons maple syrup

2 tablespoons tahini

1 teaspoon anchovy paste

1 teaspoon toasted sesame oil

Freshly ground black pepper

EVERYTHING ELSE

2 large heads radicchio

1 large fennel bulb

1 blood orange, supremed
(see Hot Tip on page 60)

⅓ cup walnuts, toasted and
roughly chopped

1 sheet nori

Kosher salt

Freshly ground black pepper

To make the dressing, combine the miso, rice wine vinegar, lemon juice, and 2 tablespoons hot water in a medium jar. Cover tightly and shake until the miso is dissolved. Add the olive oil, maple syrup, tahini, anchovy paste, and sesame oil and shake again. Season with pepper. (The dressing can be stored in an airtight container in the fridge for up to 2 weeks.)

Core the radicchio and remove any wilted outer leaves, then separate the leaves and tear into large, bite-size pieces.

Trim, halve, and core the fennel (reserve the fennel fronds for garnish), then very thinly slice the fennel using a mandoline or very sharp knife. (The fennel can be prepared a few hours ahead of time and held in a bowl of ice water, then patted dry when ready to use.)

Combine the radicchio and fennel on a shallow platter, drizzle with the dressing, and toss. Add the blood orange, squeezing in any remaining juice from the core, and the walnuts and gently toss. Crush the nori into fine pieces and sprinkle atop the salad. Garnish with the reserved fennel fronds, season with salt and pepper to taste, and serve.

Try With Tuna with Roasted Cherry and Caper Salsa (page 139).

GARLICKY CAPRESE
with Hoisin Buttermilk Ranch

SERVES 6

When tomatoes join forces with anything "caprese" (cue mozz and basil), well, let's just say my summer romance blooms into true devotion. This recipe runs with that iconic combination and adds a tangy and creamy umami-packed buttermilk dressing—the addition of hoisin adds a depth of flavor that brings out both the sweet and savory of the tomatoes. A sprinkle of crispy garlic, found often in Chinese, Thai, and Vietnamese cooking, adds texture and crunch.

CRISPY GARLIC

20 garlic cloves, peeled and minced

1 cup neutral oil

HOISIN BUTTERMILK RANCH

¼ cup sour cream

¼ cup buttermilk

2 tablespoons Kewpie mayonnaise

1 tablespoon hoisin

1 teaspoon fresh lemon juice

½ teaspoon sriracha

¼ cup minced chives

1 tablespoon minced dill fronds

Kosher salt

Freshly ground black pepper

EVERYTHING ELSE

2 pints heirloom cherry tomatoes, cut in half

1 (8-ounce) ball burrata, torn into large, bite-size pieces

Extra-virgin olive oil, for finishing

½ cup basil leaves

1 scallion, thinly sliced

Flaky sea salt, for finishing

Crusty bread, for serving

To make the crispy garlic, put the garlic in a medium skillet and add the oil. The oil should cover the garlic; if needed, add a touch more oil. Turn the heat to medium and fry the garlic, stirring frequently and turning the heat down to medium-low if the oil foams up too much, until golden brown, 6 to 8 minutes. Turn off the heat and let the garlic sit for another 1 to 2 minutes until deep golden brown.

Drain the garlic in a fine-mesh sieve set over a bowl and let cool completely. (The fried garlic can be made up to 1 month ahead and stored in an airtight container in the refrigerator. Store the garlic-infused oil in a separate airtight container in the refrigerator for up to 1 month and use it for cooking.)

To make the dressing, combine the sour cream, buttermilk, mayonnaise, hoisin, lemon juice, sriracha, chives, dill, ½ teaspoon salt, and ¼ teaspoon pepper in a wide-mouth jar. Cover tightly and shake vigorously until emulsified, combined, and creamy.

To serve, spread some dressing on a shallow bowl (you will have some left over), then top with the cherry tomatoes. Arrange the burrata among the tomatoes. Drizzle with a glug of olive oil. Spoon the crispy garlic atop, followed by the basil and scallion. Finish with flaky sea salt and serve with bread alongside. .

Hot Tip If you don't want to fry your own garlic, you can buy it in large jars in most Asian grocery stores or online.

Try With Sweet and Sour Sticky Ribs with Citrus Peanut Gremolata (page 182).

Really Green
CHOPPED SALAD

SERVES 4

It's easy being green, especially with this salad. The crunch factor is high here with apples, cucumber, and celery (ideal for those leftover stalks lurking in your fridge, which I always seem to have). As it's a chopped salad, it's perfect for those busy weekday work lunches when you have one hand holding your fork and your other hand typing an email (we've all been there, haven't we?).

VINAIGRETTE

Grated zest and juice of
1 lemon (about 1 teaspoon zest
and 2 tablespoons juice)

2 teaspoons apple cider
vinegar

2 teaspoons Dijon mustard

1 teaspoon honey

1 tablespoon minced dill fronds

1 small jalapeño, seeded and
minced

⅓ cup extra-virgin olive oil

Kosher salt

Freshly ground black pepper

EVERYTHING ELSE

3 celery ribs, thinly sliced on
the diagonal

1 English cucumber or 4 baby
cucumbers, halved lengthwise
and thinly sliced

1 Granny Smith apple, cored
and thinly sliced

½ cup thawed shelled
edamame

2 cups packed baby spinach
(about 2 ounces)

¼ cup roughly chopped mint
leaves, plus more for garnish

2 tablespoons roughly chopped
dill, plus more for garnish

1 avocado, peeled, pitted, and
thinly sliced

¼ cup pistachios, roughly
chopped

Flaky sea salt, for finishing

To make the vinaigrette, combine the lemon zest and juice, apple cider vinegar, Dijon, honey, dill, jalapeño, and olive oil in a small jar. Season with a good pinch of kosher salt and pepper, cover tightly, and shake vigorously to incorporate.

Combine the celery, cucumber, apple, edamame, spinach, mint, and dill in a serving bowl, drizzle with some of the vinaigrette, and gently toss to combine. Top with the avocado and pistachios and drizzle with more vinaigrette. Garnish with additional mint and dill, finish with flaky sea salt, and serve.

Remix! If in season, swap out the edamame for fresh shelled peas (blanch them in boiling water for 1½ minutes, then plunge in a bowl filled with ice water).

Another Remix! Try adding crumbled feta or blue cheese, shaved Pecorino Romano, cubed ham, or chopped hard-boiled eggs.

BEETS *and* BLACKBERRIES
with Orange Blossom Labneh and Calamansi Vinaigrette

SERVES 4 TO 6

With its deep jewel tones, it's a pretty salad to look at, but believe me, it's even better to eat.

A few ingredient notes: First, calamansi is a citrus fruit often used in Southeast Asian (especially Filipino) cuisine, and it tastes like a mix of lime and orange. You can find bottled or canned calamansi juice in most Asian markets. Second, if you can find smaller beets, use those as they'll roast faster. For an even quicker take, buy pre-roasted beets—usually available in an 8-ounce package in the produce section. Lastly, note that I'm not using orange extract but orange blossom water, which has a softer, more floral flavor profile than extract. It's available in most larger supermarkets, Asian or Middle Eastern grocers, and online and can be stored for a while in the pantry. Add a splash to any recipe where you want to highlight a citrus flavor.

3 pounds beets, peeled (see Hot Tip)

1 tablespoon extra-virgin olive oil

Kosher salt

Freshly ground black pepper

1 cup labneh

1 tablespoon orange blossom water

1 tablespoon calamansi juice

1 tablespoon orange juice

½ pint blackberries, halved if large

¼ cup mint leaves

1 teaspoon grated lime zest

Flaky sea salt

CALAMANSI VINAIGRETTE

2 tablespoons calamansi juice

2 tablespoons rice wine vinegar

1 tablespoon white wine vinegar

1 teaspoon fresh lime juice

½ teaspoon ground coriander

½ cup extra-virgin olive oil

Kosher salt

Freshly ground black pepper

Preheat the oven to 400°F.

Put the beets in a small baking dish. Drizzle with the olive oil and season well with kosher salt and pepper. Cover with aluminum foil and roast for 45 to 60 minutes, or until tender; the tip of a knife should easily slide into the flesh. If your beets are larger, you may need to roast for 20 to 25 more minutes. Let cool.

Meanwhile, make the vinaigrette. In a large bowl, whisk together the calamansi juice, rice wine vinegar, white wine vinegar, lime juice, and coriander. Stream in the olive oil while whisking and continue to whisk until emulsified. Season with kosher salt and pepper. (The vinaigrette can be made ahead and stored in an airtight container in the fridge for up to 2 weeks.)

Cut the beets into bite-size wedges, add to the bowl, and gently mix to coat in the vinaigrette.

In a small bowl, combine the labneh, orange blossom water, calamansi juice, and orange juice. Season with kosher salt and pepper and whisk to combine.

To serve, swirl the labneh on a serving platter, then top with the dressed beets and blackberries. Drizzle a bit more vinaigrette atop, along with a glug of olive oil. Garnish with the mint leaves, finish with the lime zest and flaky sea salt, and serve.

Hot Tip I prefer to peel beets (using a vegetable peeler) before roasting them as I find it to be a less messy process. However, you may roast them with their skins on and remove after. Either way, wear rubber kitchen gloves or food prep gloves to prevent your hands from turning a lovely shade of purple.

Remix! If you can't find calamansi juice, use a mix of half orange and half lime juice.

WINTRY PANZANELLA
with Roasted Carrot Ginger Dressing

SERVES 4 TO 6

I love the carrot ginger dressing on my salad when I'm out having sushi, and I love it even more here—where I roast the carrots beforehand. An extra step to be sure, but the reward for that effort (if you can even call it that) is a sweet, mellowed depth of flavor that creates quite a luxurious creamy dressing. Even better, two sheet pans and the oven do most of the heavy lifting.

Panzanella is a classic Italian summer salad that traditionally combines stale bread pieces with tomatoes. Here, I've given it the cool-weather treatment with tender caramelized roasted veg—the perfect pairing with the sweet, gingery pop of the dressing. Does this dish go in the salad section? Unsure, because it straddles the line—and in all the best ways possible—as it can be a starter but is also substantial enough to hold its own as a side dish.

3 cups ½-inch diced butternut squash (see Hot Tip)

8 ounces brussels sprouts, trimmed and quartered

1 medium red onion, cut into 1-inch chunks

1 lemon, thinly sliced into rounds

1 tablespoon fennel seeds

1 teaspoon ground ginger

Kosher salt

Freshly ground black pepper

4 tablespoons extra-virgin olive oil, divided

3 cups bite-size (torn) pieces sourdough bread (about half a small boule)

2 medium carrots, cut into 1-inch pieces

⅓ cup cashews

1 small shallot, roughly chopped

⅓ cup neutral oil

⅓ cup rice wine vinegar

1 (1-inch) piece fresh ginger, peeled and roughly chopped

1 garlic clove, peeled

1 tablespoon soy sauce

1 tablespoon honey

2 cups baby kale

¼ cup coarsely chopped flat-leaf parsley

Preheat the oven to 450°F with racks in the center and lower positions. Place a rimmed baking sheet in the oven to preheat at the same time.

In a large bowl, combine the butternut squash, brussels sprouts, red onion, lemon, fennel seeds, and ground ginger. Season with salt and pepper and toss with 2 tablespoons of the olive oil to evenly coat.

(recipe continues)

Carefully remove the baking sheet from the oven and add the prepared vegetables in a single layer. Roast on the center oven rack for 35 minutes, tossing halfway through, or until the vegetables are tender and slightly charred in spots.

Meanwhile, put the sourdough pieces on one half of a second rimmed baking sheet and the carrots on the other half. Toss each side with 1 tablespoon olive oil, ensuring the bread and carrots stay separate, and season with salt and pepper. Place this second baking sheet on the lower oven rack and roast for 20 minutes, or until the bread is pale golden brown and the carrots are tender and caramelized.

While everything is roasting, put the cashews in a small bowl and fill with hot water. Let soak for 10 minutes, then drain.

To make the dressing, combine the roasted carrots, cashews, shallot, neutral oil, rice wine vinegar, ⅓ cup cold water, ginger, garlic, soy sauce, and honey in a blender and puree until smooth. Season well with salt and pepper.

To serve, combine the roasted vegetables and sourdough on a serving platter, add the baby kale and parsley, then toss with the dressing. Leftover dressing will keep in an airtight container in the fridge for up to 2 weeks.

Try With Big Beautiful Beef Stew (page 166).

Hot Tip Save time and buy precut cubed butternut squash.

Remix! Add sliced cooked chicken breast or cubed tofu to make it a main.

Another Remix! Lose the squash 'n' sprouts and summer-ize it with heirloom tomatoes or cherry tomatoes.

PARM BROCCOLI
with Honey Chili Crisp

SERVES 4

Broccoli was the unsung backup dancer at the family dinner table when I was growing up: steamed, slightly bland, saltless (health-conscious Mom did not use salt), and served weekly to absolutely no applause. It was eaten because it was a vegetable, and that was really it. Now, the magic of roasting the ever-dependable broccoli transforms it into something beautiful—the florets get crunchy, the stems tender, and the caramelization of all of it creates a perfect bite. I've upped things with the nuanced heat of chili crisp, the sweetness of honey, and, for a final flourish, a shower of freshly grated parm. Backup dancer no more!

1 pound broccoli (about 2 small heads)

1 tablespoon extra-virgin olive oil

Kosher salt

Freshly ground black pepper

½ cup packed freshly grated parmesan

2 tablespoons chili crisp

1 tablespoon honey

1 teaspoon grated lemon zest

Flaky sea salt, for finishing

Preheat the oven to 450°F with a rack in the center position. Line a rimmed baking sheet with parchment paper.

Trim the broccoli and cut it into long florets, incorporating as much of the tender stems—say, 2 to 3 inches—as possible. Put the broccoli on the prepared baking sheet, drizzle with the olive oil, and season with ½ teaspoon kosher salt and ¼ teaspoon pepper. Toss to coat, then spread out in a single layer.

Roast the broccoli for 10 minutes, until bright green and just starting to brown in spots. Toss, then sprinkle an even layer of parmesan across the entire baking sheet and roast for another 10 to 15 minutes, or until the parmesan is a crisp golden brown and the broccoli is tender and charred in spots. Remove from the oven and let sit for 1 to 2 minutes. Drizzle with the chili crisp and honey, then use metal tongs to break up the crispy parm from the baking sheet and gently toss it with the broccoli.

Transfer to a serving platter, finish with the lemon zest and some flaky sea salt, and serve.

Hot Tip Use a Microplane to grate the parmesan.

Try With Braised Soy and Black Garlic Short Ribs (page 174).

Remix! Try this recipe with broccoli or broccolini!

ROASTED BRUSSELS SPROUTS *with Grapefruit*

SERVES 4 TO 6

You'll see that I add citrus to a lot of recipes in this book. Whether it's a squeeze of lemon juice, grated lime zest, or sections of grapefruit (as is the case here), citrus adds a floral brightness and acidity without the sharpness of vinegar. The tart sweetness of grapefruit is the perfect pairing for earthy brussels sprouts that have been dressed in a powerhouse of a vinaigrette that's sweet, savory, and funky.

2 pounds brussels sprouts, trimmed and cut in half if large

2 tablespoons neutral oil

1 teaspoon ground coriander

½ teaspoon ground cardamom

Kosher salt

Freshly ground black pepper

2 large grapefruits, supremed (see Hot Tip)

¼ cup chopped cilantro leaves, plus more for garnish

Mint leaves, for garnish

Basil leaves, for garnish

Flaky sea salt, for finishing

VINAIGRETTE

2 tablespoons fish sauce

1 tablespoon maple syrup

1 teaspoon soy sauce

1 teaspoon rice wine vinegar

1 bird's eye chili, thinly sliced (optional)

Preheat the oven to 450°F. Line a rimmed baking sheet with parchment paper.

Put the brussels sprouts on the prepared baking sheet, including any leaves—they'll get crispy and wonderful. Drizzle with the oil, sprinkle with the coriander and cardamom, season with kosher salt and pepper, and toss until evenly coated. Arrange in a single layer with as many as you feel like cut side down (but no need to go nuts here) and roast for 25 minutes, or until the brussels sprouts are tender and deeply browned in spots.

Meanwhile, make the vinaigrette. In a large bowl, combine the fish sauce, maple syrup, soy sauce, rice wine vinegar, and chili (if using) and whisk to combine.

Add the grapefruit segments to the same bowl, then squeeze any juice from the remaining grapefruit core over the bowl. Season with kosher salt and pepper and gently toss to combine, using a spoon to break up the grapefruit sections a bit.

Add the brussels sprouts to the bowl, along with the cilantro, and quicky toss a few times to coat. Immediately transfer to a serving platter, garnish with cilantro, mint, and basil, then finish with flaky sea salt and serve immediately.

Hot Tip To supreme a citrus fruit, use a paring knife to cut away the rind and pith to expose the flesh, then cut out each individual segment, leaving the membrane behind—make sure you are using a sharp knife and go slowly. Remember to always squeeze any juice out of the remaining core once you're done.

CHARRED CABBAGE
with Hoisin Tahini Caesar

SERVES 6 TO 8

My love for all things Caesar is profound and true (and I know I'm not alone on this), and here the addition of hoisin and tahini brings a nutty richness and depth of flavor that pairs up perfectly with charred cabbage wedges.

1 large head green cabbage, cut into 8 wedges with root end attached

4 tablespoons extra-virgin olive oil, for drizzling

Kosher salt

Freshly ground black pepper

1 tablespoon fennel seeds

HOISIN TAHINI CAESAR

½ cup Greek yogurt

3 tablespoons tahini

Juice of 1 lemon

2 tablespoons Kewpie mayonnaise

2 tablespoons extra-virgin olive oil

1 tablespoon Dijon mustard

2 teaspoons hoisin sauce

2 teaspoons anchovy paste

¼ cup finely grated Pecorino Romano

Kosher salt

Freshly ground black pepper

EVERYTHING ELSE

2 teaspoons extra-virgin olive oil

¼ cup panko

1 tablespoon toasted sesame seeds

1 teaspoon grated lemon zest

Chopped dill fronds and chives, for garnish

Flaky sea salt, for finishing

Preheat the oven to 450°F with a rack in the center position. Line a rimmed baking sheet with parchment paper.

Spread out the cabbage wedges on the prepared baking sheet and drizzle with olive oil. Season with kosher salt and pepper and roast for about 20 minutes, or until the wedges are tender and charred on the edges. Flip, sprinkle with the fennel seeds, season again with kosher salt and pepper, and continue to roast for an additional 20 minutes, or until the edges are charred, the cabbage is tender, and a knife inserted into the root end slides in easily.

Meanwhile, make the dressing. In a large bowl, combine the Greek yogurt, tahini, lemon juice, mayonnaise, olive oil, mustard, hoisin, anchovy paste, and Pecorino Romano. Season with kosher salt and pepper and whisk until smooth.

In a small skillet, heat the olive oil over medium heat. Add the panko and sesame seeds and toast, stirring frequently, until deep golden brown, 2 to 3 minutes. Remove the pan from the heat and stir in the lemon zest.

Arrange the cabbage on a serving platter and drizzle with the dressing. Sprinkle the sesame panko atop, then garnish with dill and chives. Finish with flaky sea salt and serve.

Try With Big Beautiful Beef Stew (page 166).

CAULIFLOWER MARBELLA

SERVES 4

This meat-free—but just as satisfying—dish was inspired by the *Silver Palate*'s iconic Chicken Marbella. Cauliflower, roasted until tender and caramelized, gets enrobed in a vibrant sauce of white wine, red wine vinegar, olives, prunes, and honey for a frankly mouthwatering situation. Briny, sweet, salty, herbaceous—so easy to make and even easier to eat.

1 large head cauliflower (2 to 2½ pounds)

⅓ cup plus 3 tablespoons extra-virgin olive oil, divided

Kosher salt

Freshly ground black pepper

4 bay leaves

½ cup red wine vinegar

4 garlic cloves, minced

½ cup pitted Spanish green olives

¼ cup capers, plus 1 tablespoon brining liquid

2 tablespoons dried oregano

1 tablespoon honey

¼ cup dry white wine

1 cup halved prunes

2 tablespoons chopped flat-leaf parsley

Flaky sea salt, for finishing

Preheat the oven to 450°F with a rack in the center position. Line a rimmed baking sheet with parchment paper.

Cut the cauliflower into ½- to ¾-inch slabs, then cut the slabs into 1-inch florets. Trim the stem and cut into ½- to ¾-inch slices. Put the cauliflower on the prepared baking sheet and drizzle with 3 tablespoons of the olive oil, then season with 1 teaspoon kosher salt and ¼ teaspoon pepper. Spread out the cauliflower in a single layer and roast for 20 to 25 minutes, or until golden, tender, and charred in spots.

In the meantime, heat the remaining ⅓ cup olive oil in a medium to large skillet over medium-low heat. Add the bay leaves and cook for 5 minutes, then remove and discard the bay leaves. Add the red wine vinegar, garlic, olives, capers, oregano, and honey, turn the heat up to medium-high, and simmer for 2 to 3 minutes, stirring constantly, until the mixture is emulsified and slightly reduced. Add the wine and caper brining liquid and bring to a boil, then turn the heat down to a simmer, stirring occasionally and using the back of a wooden spoon to crush some of the olives. Add the prunes and simmer for 3 to 4 minutes, or until the sauce is thickened slightly. Season with kosher salt and pepper to taste.

Arrange the cauliflower on a serving platter and pour the sauce atop. Garnish with the parsley, finish with flaky sea salt, and serve.

Hot Tip Slicing the cauliflower into slabs first creates flat sides—which means more contact with the hot sheet pan, which means more browning.

Try With Cornish Game Hens with Garlicky Mushroom Rice (page 161).

Remix! Try it with broccoli instead of cauliflower!

SCALLION CORN PANCAKES
with Five-Spice Honey

SERVES 4 TO 6

Listen, this recipe is technically more of a snack item, but it's so packed with veggie goodness I thought it would be better here in the veg chapter. In any case, a stack of these pancakes, solo or with some scrambled eggs on the side, and brunch is served. Though I should mention that they are equally delicious reheated as a late-night snack. So, win-win in my book.

2 lap cheong links, diced

1 cup all-purpose flour

1½ teaspoons baking powder

1 teaspoon sugar

Kosher salt

Freshly ground black pepper

¾ cup seltzer

2 ears corn, shucked and kernels cut off (about 1½ cups)

½ cup shredded cheddar

1 Thai red chili, finely minced (optional)

1 bunch scallions, thinly sliced

Neutral oil, for frying

⅓ cup honey
½ teaspoon five-spice powder

Furikake, for garnish

Flaky sea salt, for finishing

In a large cast-iron or other heavy skillet, cook the lap cheong over medium heat for about 3 minutes, or until tender and just starting to brown in the corners. Use a slotted spoon to transfer to a small bowl, leaving the fat behind in the pan. Set the lap cheong aside and let cool.

In a medium bowl, whisk together the flour, baking powder, sugar, 1 teaspoon kosher salt, and ½ teaspoon pepper. Stir in the seltzer with a wooden spoon or spatula until combined, then fold in the corn, cheddar, lap cheong, and chili (if using). Reserve 2 tablespoons scallions for garnish and mix the rest into the bowl.

Add 1 tablespoon neutral oil to the fat in the pan and heat over medium heat. Using a ¼-cup measuring cup, add the batter to the pan, pressing down gently to flatten each pancake to about ½ inch thick. Cook for 4 minutes per side, or until deep golden brown, working in batches and adding more oil as needed.

In a small bowl, stir together the honey and five-spice powder until combined.

Drizzle the cakes with the five-spice honey, sprinkle with furikake, finish with flaky sea salt, and garnish with the reserved scallions. Serve hot.

GREEN BEANS
with Pickled Things

SERVES 4 Why boil when you can roast? My childhood memories of anemic, limp, and watery green beans have finally been cast away for good, because once I discovered the magic of roasting them, my green bean relationship changed from UGH to AAAH. Their flavor intensifies when caramelization happens, which means bigger green bean flavor for you. I've paired them with briny pickled things, which are so easy to make for a super bright bite. Adding golden raisins to the pickling process plumps them up and adds a lovely sweet balance.

PICKLED THINGS

¼ cup rice wine vinegar

½ teaspoon chili flakes

½ teaspoon sugar

Kosher salt

⅓ cup thinly sliced red onion

3 tablespoons golden raisins

EVERYTHING ELSE

1 pound green beans, trimmed

1 tablespoon extra-virgin olive oil, plus more for finishing

Kosher salt

Freshly ground black pepper

½ cup pitted green olives

¼ cup roughly chopped roasted pistachios

1 teaspoon grated lemon zest

Flaky sea salt, for finishing

In a small bowl, combine the rice wine vinegar, chili flakes, sugar, ½ teaspoon kosher salt, and ¼ cup warm water and mix well. Add the red onion and raisins and make sure they are submerged. Set aside at room temperature for 1 hour, or until the onion is tender and the raisins are plump (or cover and refrigerate for up to 24 hours).

Preheat the oven to 400°F with a rack in the center position. Line a rimmed baking sheet with parchment paper.

On the prepared baking sheet, toss the green beans with the olive oil, ½ teaspoon kosher salt, and ¼ teaspoon pepper. Spread out the green beans in a single layer and roast for 16 to 20 minutes, or until tender and slightly charred in spots.

Arrange the green beans on a platter. Top with the pickled red onion and raisins, along with 1 tablespoon of the pickling liquid. Break apart the olives with your hands (or roughly chop with a knife) and add to the plate, along with the pistachios. Finish with a glug of olive oil, the lemon zest, and some flaky sea salt and serve.

Try With Hoisin Honey Roast Chicken (page 155).

CHARRED CARROTS
with Gochujang Honey Butter
(aka Gala Carrots)

SERVES 4

This recipe came to me under duress. It was the first Monday in May, in the early 2000s, and as an up-and-coming fashion designer I had been invited to the Met Gala. The blindingly high-octane glamour and setting were intoxicatingly unreal. That, combined with the gilded gloss of the outfits worn by very fancy people, preening in the riotous orbit of the paparazzi, was both beautiful and terrifying. I was to attend alone—no model or starlet to accompany and fuss over—just me, sweating in my tux. I got through the evening, and instead of going to the after-parties, I hailed a cab and escaped home.

Starving, I kicked off my patent loafers and opened my fridge to find a bunch of week-old carrots in a bag. I turned on the oven, tossed those lonely carrots with olive oil, and threw them in the oven to roast. Little did I know that I had turned the oven not to 400°F but to 450°F. Well, happy mistake because the carrots were tender, deliciously charred in spots, and caramelized. I drizzled honey and gochujang on them and, leaning against my kitchen counter at 11 p.m., happily ate them all up. Sweet, spicy, crunchy, tender perfection. It was my own after-party, and at that moment I wouldn't have wanted it any other way. And so, gala carrots were born. I've made this dish hundreds of times—each time as delicious as that first night.

This recipe doesn't require duress (or fancy dress, for that matter)—in reality all you need is some fridge and pantry staples, a raring-hot oven, and a watchful eye. While I ate this as my main course post–Met Gala, rest assured that these carrots will be the perfect side dish to any dinner all year long, including the first Monday in May.

72

1½ pounds carrots (about 15 carrots), trimmed (see Hot Tip)

1 tablespoon extra-virgin olive oil

Kosher salt

Freshly ground black pepper

2 tablespoons honey

2 tablespoons unsalted butter

2 tablespoons gochujang

½ cup roughly chopped toasted hazelnuts (optional)

1 teaspoon grated orange zest

Flaky sea salt, for finishing

Flat-leaf parsley leaves, for garnish (optional)

Preheat the oven to 450°F with a rack in the top third of the oven. Line a rimmed baking sheet with parchment paper.

Cut any larger carrots in half lengthwise and put them all on the prepared baking sheet. Drizzle with the olive oil, season with 1 teaspoon kosher salt and ½ teaspoon pepper, and use your hands to mix so that the carrots are evenly coated, then spread out in a single layer. Roast for 20 to 25 minutes, tossing the carrots and rotating the pan halfway through, or until the carrots are tender and just charred in spots.

While the carrots are roasting, combine the honey, butter, and gochujang in a small microwave-safe bowl and microwave for 1 minute, or until the butter is melted. Whisk to combine.

When the carrots are done, remove them from the oven and immediately pour the gochujang mixture atop, then use tongs to toss so the carrots are thoroughly coated. Transfer to a serving platter, sprinkle the hazelnuts atop, if using, finish with the orange zest and flaky sea salt, and garnish with fresh parsley, if you like. Serve warm or at room temperature.

Hot Tip Use multicolored carrots if they're available for an extra-pleasing presentation.

Try With Chicken Thighs with Miso Romesco and Shallots (page 150) or Crispy Tofu with Charred Scallion Pesto (page 197).

FANCY MUSHROOMS
and CREAMY BEANS
with Citrus Brown Butter

SERVES 4

Gourmet mushrooms are usually packaged together at the grocery store, but ideally you can find them separately at better grocery stores or the farmers' market as they'll be fresher (but this is not necessary). A mix of oyster, shiitake, maitake, royal trumpet is great. I love to serve this dish for company as a main course, along with a salad and a baguette, for the easiest but so highly satisfying vegetarian lunch.

FANCY MUSHROOMS

2 pounds fancy mushrooms, cut or torn into large, bite-size pieces

3 garlic cloves, thinly sliced

3 tablespoons extra-virgin olive oil

6 thyme sprigs

2 rosemary sprigs

Kosher salt

Freshly ground black pepper

CREAMY WHITE BEANS

2 (15-ounce) cans cannellini beans, drained and rinsed

¼ cup extra-virgin olive oil

1 garlic clove, peeled

2 teaspoons soy sauce

2 teaspoons rice wine vinegar

Kosher salt

Freshly ground black pepper

EVERYTHING ELSE

5 tablespoons unsalted butter

½ teaspoon ground cardamom

2 teaspoons grated orange zest

1 teaspoon orange juice

Shaved Pecorino Romano, for finishing

Flaky sea salt, for finishing

Flat-leaf parsley leaves, for garnish

Crusty bread, for serving

Preheat the oven to 450°F with a rack in the center position. Place a rimmed baking sheet in the oven to preheat at the same time.

In a very large bowl, combine the mushrooms, garlic, oil, thyme, and rosemary. Season with 2 teaspoons kosher salt and ½ teaspoon pepper. Carefully spread the mushrooms onto the heated baking sheet in an even layer—you should hear a sizzle as they hit the pan! Roast, tossing once and rotating the pan halfway through, for 20 to 25 minutes, or until the mushrooms are browned, tender, and crisp on the edges. If the mushrooms are not sufficiently crisp at this point, remove the thyme and rosemary sprigs, turn the broiler on high, and broil for 3 to 4 minutes, but watch closely so they don't burn. *(recipe continues)*

Meanwhile, to make the creamy white beans, combine the beans, olive oil, garlic, soy sauce, rice wine vinegar, and 1 tablespoon water in a food processor and puree until smooth. Season with 1 teaspoon kosher salt and ¼ teaspoon pepper. Spread the puree onto a serving platter or shallow bowl.

When the mushrooms are done, in a small pot, melt the butter in a small saucepan over medium heat for 5 to 6 minutes, or until the butter has foamed up, brown bits form at the bottom of the saucepan, and the butter is nutty and fragrant. Remove the saucepan from the heat and whisk in the cardamom, orange zest, and juice.

Top the white beans with the warm mushrooms and drizzle the brown butter atop. Finish with Pecorino Romano and flaky sea salt, garnish with parsley, and serve with bread alongside.

Remix! Make the creamy beans into a soup instead! Combine your creamy beans with 1½ to 2 cups water or stock and a splash of milk in a blender and puree until smooth, then season to taste with salt and pepper.

Rice Bowl

What can I say about rice? Rice is everything! Rice is warm, fluffy security; rice is tender, toothsome consistency. A bowl of rice can even symbolize hopes and dreams. Auntie May—my mom's older sister—recalls that during WWII, Grandma and Grandpa left Hong Kong and took the family to Macao to live—Mom was 4 and Auntie May was 5. There were 12 people to feed and food was scarce, so meals would be a small bit of salted fish with some ginger that would be put on top of rice, and then maybe a small bit of vegetables. Everyone tightly held their bowl and ate slowly to savor each bite. So when each day was faced with the grim uncertainty of war, a bowl of rice was the one constant. So loyal and ever-present. Indeed, though under much different circumstances, we had it for every dinner growing up, no matter if we were eating Chinese steamed pork cake with salted fish or French beef bourguignon. Mom always made sure we finished our rice—the wartime memory of that single precious bowl of rice in her hands never left her. She would tell us about the old Chinese superstition that if you don't finish all the rice in your bowl, your future spouse will have a bad complexion—each piece of leftover rice represents a blemish on their face. Marital complexion threats aside, there's so much more to be done with the mighty rice. Besides serving as that steaming stalwart backdrop for more flashy fare, the bowlscape of rice takes center stage with my Golden Fried Rice (page 82) and Crispy Upside-Down Fried Rice (page 85).

ON FRIED RICE

I was going to wax poetic about my deep, intense love for fried rice, but I'll spare you the histrionics. Rice, in general, is my staff of life, but fried rice is all of that and so much more. While it's a key player in my monthly meal playbook, it's truly nothing fancy. As with so many things in life, the sum is greater than its parts: some day-old leftover rice, some leftover vegetables, a few eggs, and if you have it, some tofu or meat, a dash of soy sauce or oyster sauce, and a *very* hot wok. And boom! Magic. All that from old rice and whatever's left in the fridge? I'll take it. The three recipes that follow are riffs on the classic, but the add-ins are endlessly changeable. Much like accessories on a little black dress, feel free to change things up as the mood strikes. A recipe is barely needed for good basic fried rice; here are my guidelines:

1. Use cold, day-old rice. It's a must. Freshly cooked rice has too much moisture.
2. Your wok or pan needs to be raring hot. In general, nonstick pans aren't good to use as they can only tolerate up to medium heat, so use a heavy skillet—cast iron or stainless are great here. Use a neutral oil with a high smoke point, like avocado oil or grapeseed oil (olive oil won't cut it here, as it'll start to smoke).
3. Cook your eggs first, then remove from the pan. I prefer to cook in a single layer and then cut into ribbons.
4. Sauté all your add-ins—start with some ginger, then onions and garlic, followed by whatever you have from the fridge. Make sure everything is cut into small, uniform-ish, bite-size pieces, and remember you're merely heating these things back up—everything's already cooked. Then stir in the rice. Fold the eggs back in.
5. Season to your liking with a mix of soy sauce and oyster sauce and finish with a light glug of toasted sesame oil.
6. Stir in any herbs, then let sit for a few minutes undisturbed to create that crisp bottom.
7. This should all happen within 5 or so minutes. Eat up!

Golden **FRIED RICE**

SERVES 4 TO 6 Frankly, I'm all for food that makes you smile. Here, folding egg yolks into the cold rice adds not only a mood-lifting hue but also richness. While the possibilities for additions are almost endless (it's fried rice, after all), I've opted for tender caramelized roasted butternut squash and sweet corn to brighten things up so much you'll be grinning from ear to ear.

1 small butternut squash, peeled, seeded, and cut into ½-inch dice (about 4 cups)

2 tablespoons plus 2 teaspoons neutral oil, divided

Kosher salt

Freshly ground black pepper

2 large eggs, plus 6 large egg yolks (see Hot Tip)

4 cups cold day-old cooked jasmine rice

2 teaspoons Shaoxing wine

1 (½-inch) piece ginger, grated

2 garlic cloves, minced

½ teaspoon ground turmeric

2 scallions, thinly sliced, white and green parts separated

1½ cups corn kernels (from 2 to 3 ears corn)

1 teaspoon sugar

2 tablespoons minced chives, plus more for garnish

Preheat the oven to 425°F. Line a rimmed baking sheet with parchment paper.

On the prepared baking sheet, toss the squash with 2 teaspoons of the oil, season with salt and pepper, and spread out in a single layer. Roast for 30 to 35 minutes, or until tender and golden brown around the edges.

Crack the 2 eggs into a small bowl and whisk with a fork to combine.

In a large bowl, combine the rice, 6 egg yolks, and Shaoxing wine and mix gently with a spoon or your impeccably clean hands until the rice is coated uniformly with the yolks and fluffed and the grains are not clumpy.

Heat 1 tablespoon oil in a wok or large skillet over high heat until shimmering. Add the beaten eggs and cook in a single layer until set, about 1½ minutes. Slide the eggs onto a cutting board and let cool a few minutes, then cut into ½-inch ribbons. Set aside.

Add the remaining 1 tablespoon oil to the wok, along with the ginger, garlic, turmeric, and scallion whites, and cook for 1 minute, stirring frequently, until fragrant and starting to get color. Add the corn and cook for 1 to 2 minutes, or until tender. Add the rice mixture and cook for 3 to 4 minutes, stirring gently but constantly, until the yolks are cooked. Stir in the sugar and 1 teaspoon salt along with the squash, egg ribbons, scallion greens, and chives. Transfer to a serving platter, garnish with additional chives, and serve hot.

Mix In For more protein, add chickpeas or extra-firm cubed tofu.

Try With Crispy Tofu with Charred Scallion Pesto (page 197).

Hot Tip Use the leftover egg whites to make my Lychee Lime Pavlova (page 219).

Remix! Use frozen corn and pre-cubed butternut squash to speed things up.

Cheesy Crab
FRIED RICE

SERVES 4 TO 6

I've amped up the ever-reliable clean-out-your-fridge fried rice with the addition of lump crab and the creamy pull of cheese to take it from side player to center stage.

5 to 6 cups cold day-old cooked jasmine rice

3 tablespoons gochujang

3 tablespoons oyster sauce

2 tablespoons toasted sesame oil

2 tablespoons fresh lime juice

1 tablespoon rice wine vinegar

1 teaspoon onion powder

½ teaspoon garlic powder

4 scallions, thinly sliced, green and white parts separated

Kosher salt

Ground white pepper

1 cup lump crabmeat

1 cup frozen peas

2 tablespoons unsalted butter

½ cup shredded mozzarella, divided

½ cup shredded cheddar, shredded, divided

4 slices American cheese

Toasted sesame seeds, for garnish

Preheat the oven to 375°F.

In a large bowl, combine the rice, gochujang, oyster sauce, sesame oil, lime juice, rice wine vinegar, onion powder, garlic powder, and scallion whites. Season with salt and white pepper and mix to thoroughly combine. Fold in the crabmeat and peas.

Generously butter a 10-inch cast-iron skillet or other oven-safe skillet. Add half the rice mix to the skillet, then use the back of a spatula or spoon to gently smooth it out into a flat, even layer. Leaving a small border, sprinkle on half the mozzarella and half the cheddar, then arrange the American cheese slices atop. Add the remaining rice mix, spread it out flat, and top with the remaining mozzarella and cheddar. Cover with an oven-safe lid or aluminum foil. Bake for 35 minutes.

Garnish with the scallion greens and sesame seeds and serve hot.

Remix! No crab? Swap in a tin of canned tuna.

Crispy Upside-Down
FRIED RICE

SERVES 6

Who doesn't love the crispy part of the rice? No one! Those crunchy browned morsels are prized, from paella's socarrat to Korean bibimbap, and of course my beloved Chinese fried rice (chau fan). However, they're always tucked away at the bottom. Well, I say, why not have your crispies and see them too? Drawing inspiration from Persian rice—also known as tahdig—in this recipe the rice is cooked until burnished golden brown across the bottom, then it's (carefully but swiftly) turned onto a serving platter so that beautiful crisp we all so love is in the spotlight.

Kosher salt

2 cups jasmine rice

2 tablespoons soy sauce

1 tablespoon Shaoxing rice wine

½ teaspoon ground turmeric

3 tablespoons plain yogurt

3 tablespoons neutral oil, divided

2 large eggs, beaten

Freshly ground black pepper

½ cup yellow or white onion, diced

1 garlic clove, minced

1½ cups frozen peas and carrots, thawed

2 scallions, chopped, plus more for garnish

3 tablespoons unsalted butter

½ cup roughly chopped roasted peanuts

Chopped flat-leaf parsley, for garnish

Fill a Dutch oven two-thirds with water and bring to a boil over high heat. Add ¼ cup salt.

Rinse the jasmine rice in a large bowl at least 5 times, changing the water each time and using your impeccably clean hands to agitate the rice, until the water runs almost clear, then drain. Add the rice to the Dutch oven, cover, and cook until just al dente, 6 to 7 minutes. Drain through a fine-mesh sieve, then rinse the rice with cold water to stop the cooking and drain again. Transfer to a large bowl and stir in the soy sauce, Shaoxing rice wine, and turmeric.

Scoop 1½ cups rice into a small bowl and mix with the yogurt; set aside.

While the rice is cooking, in a medium nonstick skillet, heat 1 teaspoon of the oil over medium heat. Add the eggs and season with salt and pepper. Tilt the pan to evenly coat the surface, then cover and cook until just set, about 2 minutes. Transfer the eggs to a cutting board and cut into ½-inch dice.

In the same skillet, heat another 2 teaspoons oil over medium heat. Add the onion and garlic and cook for 2 to 3 minutes, until the onion starts to brown slightly, then transfer to the Dutch oven with the remaining rice. Add the peas and carrots and scallions and stir to combine.

(recipe continues)

Wipe the skillet clean. Add the butter and remaining 2 tablespoons oil and heat over medium heat until the butter has melted. Add the rice-yogurt mixture and pat it into an even layer with a spatula or the bottom of a drinking glass. Add the remaining rice mixture from the Dutch oven, mounding it slightly toward the center. Use the handle of a wooden spoon to make six holes down to the pan surface. Cook over medium heat for 15 minutes, turning the pan a quarter turn every 4 to 5 minutes to ensure even browning. Turn the heat down to low and cook for another 15 minutes, or until the rice is set and the edges are just golden brown.

To unmold, run a spatula along the sides of the pan, then place a flat serving platter on the pan and in one swift motion, invert it. Gently lift off the pan. Garnish with the peanuts, parsley, and more scallions and serve immediately.

Hot Tip While traditional fried rice is made using day-old rice, in this recipe you'll be using freshly made rice.

Try With Famous Lemon Chicken (page 153).

One-Pot *STICKY RICE and* CHICKEN

SERVES 6

One recipe I knew I needed to include when writing this book was some kind of naw mai fan, a savory sticky rice dish that we used as our stuffing for Thanksgiving and Christmas. It's a dish that I've loved with a deep devotion since I was a little kid, when I would watch Grandma meticulously chop lap cheong with her well-worn cleaver, smell the salty funk of the soaking dried shrimp, and marvel at the floating orb-like dried black mushrooms rehydrating in water. The fact that we only ate it for Thanksgiving and Christmas is most likely the reason I loved it so. But now I make it year-round, and I love it with the addition of chicken thighs, which transforms it into naw mai gai (*gai* is Cantonese for "chicken")—for a truly comforting and convenient one-pot meal that's perfectly served in a big bowl (and for me, eaten with a spoon).

CHICKEN

2 tablespoons soy sauce

2 tablespoons oyster sauce

2 tablespoons Shaoxing wine or white wine

1 tablespoon toasted sesame oil

1 tablespoon cornstarch

1 teaspoon five-spice powder

Kosher salt

Freshly ground black pepper

6 boneless, skinless chicken thighs, cut into bite-size pieces (about 1½ pounds)

RICE AND EVERYTHING ELSE

2 cups sweet (glutinous) rice

1 cup jasmine rice

2 tablespoons neutral oil

1 small onion, diced

4 garlic cloves, minced

1 tablespoon grated fresh ginger

4 scallions, sliced, white and green parts separated

4 lap cheong links, cut into ¼-inch rounds

1 pound shiitake mushrooms, stemmed and halved (or quartered if large)

3 tablespoons soy sauce

2 teaspoons oyster sauce

3 cups low-sodium chicken stock

Kosher salt

Freshly ground black pepper

½ cup roughly chopped cilantro leaves and tender stems, plus more for garnish

In a large bowl, combine the soy sauce, oyster sauce, wine, sesame oil, cornstarch, five-spice, ½ teaspoon kosher salt, and 1 teaspoon pepper and mix well. Add the chicken and toss to coat. Cover and marinate for 15 to 20 minutes at room temperature.

Combine the glutinous rice and jasmine rice in a medium bowl and rinse with several changes of cold water until the water runs clear. Pour off as much water as possible from the bowl and set aside. *(recipe continues)*

In a Dutch oven or large skillet, heat the neutral oil over medium-high heat until shimmering. Add the onion, garlic, ginger, scallion whites, lap cheong, and mushrooms and sauté until the mushrooms are browned in spots, about 8 minutes. Stir in the soy sauce, oyster sauce, and chicken and sauté for 1 to 2 minutes, stirring constantly, until combined and the chicken has started to cook. Stir in the rice.

Pour in the stock, season with ½ teaspoon salt and ¼ teaspoon pepper, and stir to combine. Bring to a simmer, then turn the heat down to low. Cover and cook, gently stirring halfway through to ensure nothing is sticking, until the rice is tender, the chicken has cooked through, and the liquid has evaporated, 25 to 30 minutes. Remove the pot from the heat and let cool for 10 to 15 minutes.

Stir in the cilantro, garnish with the scallion greens and more cilantro, and serve.

Hot Tip This version uses fresh shiitake mushrooms, but if you have Chinese dried shiitakes (or dried shrimp for that matter)—both quite traditional in naw mai fan—go ahead and use them.

Remix! Skip the chicken and add cubed extra-firm tofu.

Cacio e Pepe
STICKY RICE *with Egg*

SERVES 2

To me, there's nothing more comforting or familiar than a bowl of rice. Every dinner from my childhood featured steamed rice, and most of the time I was the one tasked with putting on the rice before my parents returned from work. Enter this recipe—comforting, oh-so tasty, and the ideal companion to practically any dish. I've infused the flavors of the Italian classic cacio e pepe into sticky rice (also known as sweet or glutinous rice) and topped it off with a sunny-side up egg, a hit of umami from nori, and a bit of spice from togarashi. A perfect snack or side (with or without the egg), it's also the perfect base for adding salmon or roast chicken.

½ cup sweet (glutinous) rice

½ cup jasmine rice

3 tablespoons rice wine vinegar

2 teaspoons sugar

1 tablespoon extra-virgin olive oil

2 large eggs

1 cup grated Pecorino Romano, plus more for finishing

Kosher salt

Freshly ground black pepper

2 sheets nori, crushed

Toasted sesame seeds, for garnish

Togarashi, for finishing

In a medium pot, combine the sweet rice and jasmine rice and rinse with cold water 2 or 3 times, or until the water runs clear.

To add the right amount of water, place the tip of your index finger on the top of the rice and fill the pot to your first knuckle. Cover and bring to a boil over medium heat, then turn the heat down to a simmer. Cover and cook until the rice is tender, about 20 minutes. Remove the pot from the heat and let it sit for 15 to 20 minutes.

In a small bowl, whisk together the rice wine vinegar and sugar until the sugar is dissolved.

While the rice is resting, heat the olive oil in a medium skillet over medium heat. Crack the eggs in and cook sunny-side up about 2 minutes or until the whites are just set, covering the pan for the last minute to set the yolks.

Uncover the rested rice and stir in the rice wine vinegar mixture, Pecorino Romano, 1 teaspoon salt, and 1 tablespoon pepper.

Spoon the rice into bowls, top each with a fried egg, then finish with a generous amount of Pecorino Romano, along with the nori, sesame seeds, and togarashi. Serve immediately.

Rice Cake
PIZZAGNA BAKE

Pizzagna? Okay, I made that up. But yep, you can guess what it is—a combo of all-time favorites pizza and lasagna. I've ditched the traditional lasagna noodles and pizza crust for Asian rice cakes in this feed-a-crowd dish. Used in East Asian cuisines, often as a part of stir-fries, rice cakes have a tender, satisfying chew and take on flavors dreamily. In this case, the flavors are a medley of ingredients we know and love: pepperoni, sausage, tomato sauce, and mozzarella. And just like pizza or lasagna, this dish will satisfy the hungry hordes at your dinner table.

1 tablespoon extra-virgin olive oil

4 (3- to 4-ounce) spicy Italian sausages, casings removed

4 ounces sliced pepperoni, cut into quarters if large

4 garlic cloves, thinly sliced

2 tablespoons soy sauce

1 tablespoon honey

1 teaspoon chili crisp

2 scallions, thinly sliced on the diagonal, plus more for garnish

2 pounds fresh or thawed frozen rice cakes (see Hot Tip)

1 (15.5-ounce) jar marinara

Kosher salt

Freshly ground black pepper

½ cup grated cheddar

1 cup grated mozzarella

¼ cup grated parmesan

Preheat the oven to 350°F.

Heat the olive oil in a large skillet over medium-high heat. Add the sausage meat and sauté, using a wooden spoon to break it up into bite-size pieces, until browned, about 4 minutes (the sausage will finish cooking in the oven). Stir in half the pepperoni, the garlic, soy sauce, honey, chili crisp, and half the scallions and sauté for 1 minute, or until fragrant.

Add the rice cakes, breaking them up to separate as you add them. Sauté for another 2 minutes, or until just softened and browned in spots, then add the marinara and stir to combine. Season with salt and pepper.

Pour the meat mixture into a 9 × 13-inch baking dish. Sprinkle with the cheddar, then the mozzarella, then the parmesan. Dot the top with the remaining pepperoni.

Cover with aluminum foil and bake for 45 minutes. Uncover and bake for another 15 minutes, or until the cheese is golden and bubbling. Garnish with additional scallions and serve.

Hot Tip Note that we are not talking about the snacky kind of rice cakes here. In this recipe I usually use the sliced variety (nin gao in Cantonese and tteok in Korean), which come as ¼-inch-thick oval disks, as opposed to the Korean tteokbokki, which are tubular sticks, but both will work here. Find them at specialty or Asian supermarkets or online.

One-Pot CREAMY KIMCHI RISOTTO

SERVES 4 TO 6

The luxuriousness of silky, tender risotto matched with the briny bite of kimchi—all in one pot. What more do I need to say?

2 tablespoons extra-virgin olive oil

1 small onion, diced (about 1 cup)

1 cup kimchi, roughly chopped, plus ¼ cup juice from the jar

1½ teaspoons sugar

1½ cups arborio rice

Kosher salt

Freshly ground black pepper

1 cup dry white wine

4½ cups low-sodium chicken stock

1 cup freshly grated Pecorino Romano, plus more for finishing

½ cup mascarpone

Furikake, for finishing

Preheat the oven to 350°F.

Heat the olive oil in a Dutch oven over medium heat. Add the onion and sauté until just starting to soften, 4 to 5 minutes, then stir in the kimchi and sugar. Add the rice, 1 teaspoon salt, and ½ teaspoon pepper and cook, stirring, until the rice is coated with oil, 1 to 2 minutes. Add the wine and reduce for 2 minutes. Add the chicken stock, kimchi juice, and Pecorino Romano and stir to combine.

Cover and transfer to the oven. Bake for 35 minutes, or until the risotto is al dente and creamy—there will be what seems like a lot of liquid left, but don't worry! Uncover and stir in the mascarpone. Continue to stir for 1 or 2 minutes or until the risotto is creamy and most of the liquid has absorbed.

Spoon into shallow bowls, finish with furikake and additional Pecorino, and serve immediately.

Mix In Feel free to fold in canned tuna or salmon at the very end for an even more substantial dish.

Use Yer NOODLE

Noodles saved me. In 2015, when my runway collection business was closing down, I was distraught. I had wanted to be a fashion designer since the fifth grade—from that point on I was laser focused on making my dream come true. Well, the dream—though so successful from the outside—was anything but. With my childhood goal seemingly slipping away, I found myself floating adrift . . . During that time, I was so lost and totally confused, embarrassed and ashamed; I would go see movies at the movie theater on 23rd Street in Chelsea at 10 a.m. on a Wednesday because I needed to escape reality—and I would often be the only one in the theater.

It was during this time that I gravitated toward noodles. The comfort of the boiling water, the steam of the al dente noodles, the action of mixing in pesto or a jar of sauce, or even just olive oil and garlic, was how I coped. And truth be told I'd often eat almost the entire box. But it comforted me, and each subsequent time at the stove I'd refine a dish a bit more, and then maybe I'd garnish it with some sprigs of parsley. Eventually, I found myself . . . well, happy. Tender, chewy ropes of udon tethered me to what was important. Round pillows of orecchiette were the landing pad for my weary head, and those ravioli, swimming in nutty brown butter, were my little life rafts. It wasn't about finding a new dream for me; it was about waking up a dream that had always been a part of me. That part of cooking that always kept my feet on the ground and connected me to life and family.

In Chinese culture, a dish of longevity noodles is presented at every birthday. The tradition—and challenge—was to eat each strand without breaking it. The longer the noodle, the longer your life. As a kid, I was always up for the task. While Grandma would use her entire arm's length, stretching her four-foot-ten frame above the table to serve the noodles to everyone, I'd be sitting beside her, sluuuuurping away, determined to live forever so I could continue to eat more and more noodles. So, it really did happen, in a way. Noodles brought me back to life and to living when it had felt like the lights to my dreams had been turned off. It's funny how food can do that. This chapter noodles around with one of the most versatile and varied pantry staples for recipes that come together quickly to be your lifeline on a hungry Wednesday at 6:30 p.m. From on-the-fly Noodles with Tomatoes and XO Butter (page 113) to a generous pot of creamy Lemony One-Pot Mac and Cheese (page 109), let's celebrate and savor each and every long sluuuurpy strand.

UDON *with*
Charred Sardines and Pecorino

SERVES 4

When hunger collides with a lack of patience (let's be real, that's most times for me), noodles become the pantry superhero. In fact, the beauty of this quick dish lies in the fact that most ingredients are pantry and fridge staples, each one bursting with bold umami flavor. In the ten minutes it takes to cook the noods, the rest of the ingredients are waiting and ready to join the party. I love udon for its characteristic springy chew, but don't hesitate to sub in ramen (or even spaghetti in a pinch).

1 pound dried udon noodles

1 tablespoon neutral oil

8 ounces mixed mushrooms, torn or cut into bite-size pieces if large (see Hot Tip)

1 (4- to 5-ounce) tin sardines in olive oil

2 tablespoons chili crisp, or more to taste

1 tablespoon oyster sauce

Kosher salt

Freshly ground black pepper

3 tablespoons cold unsalted butter, cut into cubes

½ cup finely grated Pecorino Romano, plus more for finishing

2 scallions, thinly sliced and divided

Lemon wedges, for serving

Cook the udon according to the package instructions. Reserve ½ cup of the cooking water, then drain and rinse the noodles with cold water.

In the meantime, heat the neutral oil in a large cast-iron or other heavy skillet over medium-high heat until shimmering. Add the mushrooms and sauté, stirring frequently, until golden brown in spots and tender, 5 to 7 minutes. Add the sardines along with the oil from the can and cook, breaking them up a bit with a wooden spoon until dark brown in spots, about 2 minutes.

Remove the pan from the heat and stir in the chili crisp and oyster sauce. Season with salt and pepper. Add the noodles, reserved cooking water, butter, Pecorino Romano, and half the scallions and stir until the butter is melted and all the ingredients are fully incorporated.

Transfer to a serving bowl and finish with additional Pecorino Romano. Garnish with the remaining scallions and serve immediately, with lemon wedges alongside.

Hot Tip Use any mushrooms you like here. I love king trumpet, oyster, shiitake, and shimeji, but any kind will do.

Remix! Top with a 7-minute egg as I have here or stir in some baby spinach just until it wilts.

PEARL COUSCOUS
with Crispy Mushrooms and Anchovy Labneh

SERVES 4 TO 6

Since mushrooms are the star of this dish, skip the button mushrooms and go for a mix of shiitake, oyster, maitake, and king oyster, often packaged together as a "gourmet mix." However, if you can swing it, buy the varieties separately, as they'll be fresher than the packaged medley.

CRISPY MUSHROOMS

1 pound mixed mushrooms, halved or quartered if large

¼ cup extra-virgin olive oil, plus more for finishing

Kosher salt

Freshly ground black pepper

HERBY PEARL COUSCOUS

2 tablespoons extra-virgin olive oil, divided

2 shallots, minced (⅓ to ½ cup)

2 garlic cloves, minced

1½ cups pearl (aka Israeli) couscous

Kosher salt

Freshly ground black pepper

2½ cups low-sodium vegetable broth

½ cup roughly chopped mix of flat-leaf parsley, mint, dill, and chives, plus more for garnish

ANCHOVY LABNEH

6 to 8 canned anchovies, drained and rinsed

1½ cups labneh

1 tablespoon grated lemon zest

1 tablespoon extra-virgin olive oil

Kosher salt

Freshly ground black pepper

Preheat the oven to 450°F. Spread out the mushrooms on a rimmed baking sheet, drizzle with the olive oil, and season with ½ teaspoon salt and ¼ teaspoon pepper. Roast for 15 to 20 minutes, or until the mushrooms are tender, crisp around the edges, and browned.

Meanwhile, to make the pearl couscous, heat 1 tablespoon of the olive oil in a small pot over medium heat. Add the shallots and garlic and cook for 1 minute, or until softened and fragrant. Add the couscous, season with salt and pepper, and toast for 1 to 2 minutes, stirring frequently. Add the broth and turn the heat down to a low simmer. Cover and cook for 10 minutes, or until tender. Remove from the heat, stir in the mixed herbs and remaining 1 tablespoon olive oil, and fluff with a fork.

(recipe continues)

To make the anchovy labneh, put the anchovies on a cutting board and use the flat side of your knife to mash them into a paste. Transfer them to a small bowl and add the labneh, lemon zest, and olive oil. Season with salt and pepper and whisk until combined.

To serve, swirl a platter with the labneh, then top with the couscous and mushrooms. Drizzle with a glug of olive oil, garnish with additional herbs, and serve warm or at room temperature.

Remix! Not feeling mushrooms? This preparation is equally delicious with roasted eggplant or carrots. Or skip the veg altogether and top the labneh and couscous with grilled or roasted salmon fillets.

Easy
ROASTED GARLIC PASTA

SERVES 4

What can I say, I love a dish where the oven—and one ingredient—basically do all the work. The beauty of nutty, creamy roasted garlic combines with the earthy funk of fish sauce and anchovies, adding deep, mouthwatering back notes of yum. (Yes, I used *yum* as a noun.) In fact, I'm taking bets that those garlic-adverse folks (you know who you are, and I only judge a little) among us might convert.

2 large heads garlic

4 tablespoons extra-virgin olive oil, divided

Kosher salt

1 pound dried bucatini or other long pasta

2 tablespoons cold unsalted butter, cut into cubes

2 teaspoons anchovy paste

1 cup heavy cream

1 tablespoon fresh lemon juice

Freshly ground black pepper

1 cup finely grated Pecorino Romano, plus more for serving

1 tablespoon fish sauce

Grated lemon zest, for finishing

Preheat the oven to 350°F.

Trim the tops off the garlic heads to expose the cloves, then drizzle with 1 tablespoon of the olive oil. Wrap in an aluminum foil packet, place in a small baking dish, and roast for 1 hour, or until the cloves are very soft. Let cool, then squeeze the cloves out of their skins onto a cutting board. Use the side of your knife to create a smooth paste.

Bring a large pot of well-salted water to a boil and cook the pasta until al dente according to the package instructions. Drain, reserving 1 cup of the cooking water.

Meanwhile, in a large skillet, heat the remaining 3 tablespoons olive oil and the butter over medium heat until the butter has melted. Add the garlic paste and anchovy paste and whisk until smooth. Turn the heat down to medium-low, add the cream, and whisk to combine. Stir in the lemon juice, 1 teaspoon salt, and ½ teaspoon pepper, then add the Pecorino gradually, while whisking, and simmer for 1 to 2 minutes, or until the sauce thickens a bit.

Add the pasta to the skillet and use metal tongs to mix and coat the pasta. Add the fish sauce and reserved pasta cooking water, ¼ cup at a time, mixing to combine until a glossy sauce has formed.

Portion out into serving bowls, finish with lemon zest, and serve with more Pecorino alongside.

PASTA *alla* LAP CHEONG

SERVES 4

I spent many years traveling to Italy for work. My long days were usually spent drinking way too much espresso in a factory in the middle of nowhere doing fittings. Come dinnertime, I'd perk up because the meal—no matter where we were—was always wonderful. One evening pasta alla gricia graced our tables—a Roman classic whose magic lies in its sheer simplicity, using the time-tested alchemy of guanciale (cured pork jowl), lots of black pepper, and Pecorino Romano. Here, I've used lap cheong, the classic Chinese cured sausage, in place of the guanciale, which adds a salty-sweet note to the dish. I recommend Microplaning the Pecorino Romano—you'll want those featherweight curls as they'll ensure quick, even melting for that glossy sauce you're aiming for.

Kosher salt

1 pound rigatoni

1 tablespoon extra-virgin olive oil, plus more for finishing

7 links (about 9 ounces) lap cheong, casings removed, cut into ¼-inch dice

Freshly ground black pepper

¾ cup freshly grated Pecorino Romano, plus more for serving

Bring a large pot of well-salted water to a boil and cook the pasta a few minutes shy of al dente according to the package instructions. Drain, reserving 2 cups of the cooking water.

Meanwhile, heat the olive oil in a large cast-iron or other heavy skillet over medium heat. Add the lap cheong, turn the heat down to medium-low, and sauté until tender, crisp, and golden brown in parts, about 10 minutes. Use a slotted spoon to transfer the lap cheong to a small bowl, leaving the fat in the pan.

Turn the heat up to medium-high, add the pasta and 1 cup of the reserved pasta cooking water to the pan, and cook for 5 minutes, stirring constantly, until the pasta is al dente and a glossy sauce forms and starts to coat the pasta.

Return the lap cheong to the pan, add ½ teaspoon salt, 1 teaspoon pepper, and the Pecorino Romano, and stir to combine. If too much liquid has been absorbed, add more pasta cooking water, a little at a time, and continue to stir until incorporated.

To serve, spoon the noodles into shallow bowls, finish with a glug of olive oil, and dust with additional Pecorino Romano.

Hot Tip Since there are so few ingredients, make sure you use the best-quality dried pasta you can find—it will make a difference. Look for brands made of durum wheat semolina. I like Montebello, De Cecco, and Sfoglini.

Lemony One-Pot
MAC AND CHEESE

SERVES 6

Lemons in mac and cheese? You bet. They add a level of floral acidity that cuts—and complements—all that richness, while a subtle hit of miso adds depth of flavor. This is a one-pot wonder that uses three cheeses as well as prosciutto for the ultimate crowd-pleasing indulgence.

4 tablespoons unsalted butter

1 tablespoon yellow miso

1 teaspoon garlic powder

½ teaspoon smoked paprika

½ teaspoon chili flakes

6 tablespoons all-purpose flour

1 pound dried elbow macaroni or other short pasta

1 tablespoon soy sauce

5 cups whole milk, divided

Kosher salt

Freshly ground black pepper

3 tablespoons grated lemon zest, plus more for finishing

¼ cup fresh lemon juice

1½ cups grated Pecorino Romano

1 cup freshly grated white cheddar

1 cup frozen peas, thawed

¼ cup chopped flat-leaf parsley, plus more leaves for garnish

7 ounces mini mozzarella balls (sometimes labeled "pearls")

3 ounces prosciutto, thinly sliced and torn into bite-size pieces

Flaky sea salt, for finishing

In a large pot or Dutch oven, melt the butter over medium heat. Add the miso, garlic powder, paprika, and chili flakes and stir until combined (some miso lumps will remain, but don't worry). Add the flour and whisk until incorporated, about 30 seconds. Add the pasta, soy sauce, 4 cups of the milk, and 1 cup water. Season well with kosher salt and pepper and bring to a gentle boil, stirring constantly, then turn the heat down to a simmer. Cook, stirring frequently, for about 15 minutes, or until the pasta is just al dente (it will continue to cook off the heat). Add ½ to ¾ cup additional water as needed, ¼ cup at a time, if too much liquid has been absorbed. There should be liquid at the bottom of the pot when the pasta is done.

Stir in the lemon zest, lemon juice, Pecorino Romano, cheddar, peas, and parsley. Add the remaining 1 cup milk and stir to combine. Simmer for 1 minute, stirring, until the cheeses are fully melted. Season with kosher salt and pepper.

Remove the pot from the heat and fold in the mozzarella balls and prosciutto, then garnish with additional parsley, finish with lemon zest and flaky sea salt, and serve immediately.

Remix! Use Meyer lemons, if you can get them, for a lovely upgrade.

ORECCHIETTE
with Sausage, Chinese Broccoli, and Chili Crisp

SERVES 4

Inspired by a classic trattoria standby that features wild boar sausage, broccoli rabe, and chili flakes, here I've taken a bold turn in the form of chili crisp. It hits with a complex sweet-tangy heat that turns the flavors of the dish on its head (in a good way, of course).

1 pound dried orecchiette

2 tablespoons extra-virgin olive oil

1 teaspoon five-spice powder

1 pound spicy or sweet Italian sausage, casings removed

3 garlic cloves, sliced

1 pound Chinese broccoli (gai lan), trimmed and cut into large, bite-size pieces

Kosher salt

Freshly ground black pepper

2 tablespoons chili crisp

1 tablespoon hoisin sauce

½ cup freshly grated Pecorino Romano, plus more for serving

2 teaspoons grated lemon zest

Bring a large pot of water to a boil and cook the pasta until al dente according to the package instructions. Drain, reserving ¾ cup of the pasta cooking water.

Meanwhile, heat the olive oil in a large skillet with high sides over medium heat. Add the five-spice and toast for 30 seconds. Add the sausage and cook, using a spatula or spoon to break the meat into bite-size pieces, until browned, about 4 minutes. Add the garlic and Chinese broccoli and stir to combine. Cover and cook for 3 to 4 minutes, until the broccoli is tender. Season with salt and pepper.

Turn the heat down to low, add the pasta and reserved pasta cooking water, chili crisp, hoisin, and Pecorino Romano, and stir to combine until the pasta is coated. Season with salt and pepper. Finish with the lemon zest and serve immediately, with more Pecorino Romano alongside.

Hot Tip Feel free to use any short pasta, like penne, farfalle, or fusilli.

Remix! If you can't find Chinese broccoli, use broccolini, broccoli rabe, or Lacinato kale.

NOODLES
with Tomatoes and XO Butter

SERVES 4

Hailing from Hong Kong, XO sauce is made from dried shrimp and scallops, cured ham, and aromatics, all encapsulated in little glass jars. The flavor is richly savory, with a mouthwatering level of umami, and is the perfect shortcut for this quick ramen dish. The inspiration for this dish comes from the restaurant Chinese Tuxedo in NYC's Chinatown, where a divine fusion of XO sauce and butter in noodles caught my attention (and my taste buds). Butter's fatty richness marries perfectly with the intensity of XO sauce—a dream combo. Here, I've used super-quick-cooking ramen and tomatoes for their bright acidic sweetness. It's the perfect speedy lunch or easy dinner.

3 tablespoons unsalted butter, softened

1 tablespoon brown miso

1 (2.8-ounce) jar XO sauce

½ teaspoon chili flakes

12 ounces ramen noodles

2 teaspoons soy sauce

Kosher salt

Freshly ground black pepper

1 large ripe beefsteak or heirloom tomato, sliced into thin wedges

2 scallions, thinly sliced, plus more for garnish

In a small bowl, mix the butter, miso, XO sauce, and chili flakes and set aside.

Bring a large pot of water to a boil and cook the ramen for the shortest amount of time suggested on the package instructions for al dente. Drain, reserving ¼ cup of the pasta cooking water. Rinse the noodles with cold water, then return them to the pot.

Add the XO butter, soy sauce, salt, and ½ teaspoon pepper and use chopsticks or tongs to combine thoroughly, adding the reserved pasta cooking water, a few tablespoons at a time, until a glossy sauce has formed.

Fold in the tomato and scallions, then transfer to a serving platter or individual bowls and garnish with additional scallions. Serve immediately.

Hot Tip XO sauce is available in most Asian supermarkets or online and is a great pantry item to have on hand.

The MAINS

Growing up, I tried not to sit next to Grandma at big dinners. I know that sounds bad, but hear me out. As much as it is an honor to sit next to the matriarch of the family, it's also a curse. Whenever I sat next to her, Grandma would keep piling food on my plate, nonstop. The moment I'd pause for a break, she'd look at me with alarm. "Why are you not eating? Do you not like it? Here, have some more fish—it's so good—and some sauce for the rice. Ayyiah, eat, eat! You're too skinny. We also still have your favorite shrimp dish coming out—ayyiah, where

is it? Let me ask the waiter." I eventually learned how to mime eating—taking the smallest morsel of food with my chopsticks and chewing for an extended amount of time. As long as this motion was maintained in Grandma's peripheral vision, she'd have no cause for alarm. I would like to add that this rarely worked, and I would invariably waddle away from the table overly stuffed. The lesson here: You can't fool Grandma. These dishes are fit to be the main event for any meal, whether a Tuesday dinner after work or a Saturday party for 10. They require no miming, and you can sit next to whomever you like.

CARAMEL COD
with Fragrant Lime Coconut Rice

SERVES 4

I love caramel anything—and here we are talking specifically about the savory pantheon of caramelized Vietnamese dishes like cá kho tô (fish) and thit kho (pork). Everything is braised in a clay pot on the stove with a sweet and salty (and, frankly, mouthwatering) sauce. My riff on this leans on the oven to do all the work, and I've paired it with a coconut rice infused with the vibrant brightness of lime.

LIME COCONUT RICE

1¾ cups basmati rice

1¾ cups canned unsweetened coconut cream

Grated zest and juice of 2 limes, plus more zest for garnish

Kosher salt

EVERYTHING ELSE

1 cup light brown sugar

½ cup fish sauce

2 tablespoons soy sauce

1 teaspoon ground coriander

3 medium shallots, thinly sliced

Grated zest and juice of 3 limes, plus lime wedges for serving

3 tablespoons rice wine vinegar

1½ pounds cod fillets, cut into 4 equal portions

Kosher salt

Freshly ground black pepper

1 cup cilantro leaves and tender stems

Put the rice in a medium saucepan and rinse with cold water 2 or 3 times, until the water runs clear. Pour out as much water as possible, then stir in 1¾ cups fresh water, the coconut cream, lime juice, and ½ teaspoon salt and bring to a boil over medium heat. Turn the heat down to low, cover, and cook for about 25 minutes, or until the rice is tender. Remove the pan from the heat and let sit, covered, for 15 minutes. Add the lime zest, then fluff with a fork.

While the rice is cooking, turn the broiler on low.

In a cast-iron skillet or other ovenproof pan, combine the brown sugar and ⅓ cup water and cook over medium heat, without stirring but swirling the pan occasionally, until the sugar has dissolved, turned pale amber, and started to simmer, about 4 minutes. Add the fish sauce, soy sauce, coriander, shallots, and another ⅓ cup water and stir to combine. Simmer for 4 to 5 minutes, or until the shallots are softened. Stir in the lime zest and juice, along with the rice wine vinegar.

Season the cod fillets with salt and pepper and add them to the pan. Spoon the caramel liberally over the fillets (make sure to spoon only the sauce, as any shallots on top of the fillets will burn when broiled). Broil for 8 to 9 minutes, or until the fillets are cooked through and easily flaked with a fork.

Transfer the cod to a shallow serving bowl or platter, then spoon the sauce and shallots atop. Garnish with the cilantro and lime wedges. Transfer the rice to a serving bowl, garnish with additional lime zest, and serve alongside.

Try With Quick Pickled Cukes (page 22).

MAHI-MAHI LARB
with Grapefruit Chili Crisp

SERVES 4

This dish is inspired by the flounder larb I had at The Ordinary in Charleston, South Carolina—a super fresh seafood take on the traditional South Asian dish served in lettuce cups. With a myriad of interpretations, larb typically involves umami-packed ground meat served with a generous accompaniment of lettuces and a pile of fresh herbs. Here, mahi-mahi is marinated ceviche-style in lime juice, fish sauce, and chilis and served with a chili crisp sauce brightened up by the bittersweet tang of grapefruits, perfect for warm weather dining.

½ cup fresh lime juice

1 teaspoon fish sauce

1 small red chili, seeded and minced

3 garlic cloves, finely minced

1 small red onion, very thinly sliced (about ½ cup)

2 tablespoons roughly chopped cilantro leaves and tender stems, plus more for garnish

2 mini cucumbers, thinly sliced into rounds

Kosher salt

1 pound mahi-mahi fillets, skin removed, cut into ½-inch cubes

1 ripe but firm avocado, peeled, pitted, and diced

Romaine lettuce leaves, for serving

¼ cup mint leaves

GRAPEFRUIT CHILI CRISP

¼ cup chili crisp

1 tablespoon honey

1 grapefruit, supremed (see Hot Tip on page 60)

In a large bowl, combine the lime juice, fish sauce, red chili, garlic, red onion, cilantro, and cucumbers. Season with salt and mix well. Add the mahi-mahi and gently toss to combine. Cover and refrigerate for 30 to 60 minutes, or until the fish has turned opaque.

To make the grapefruit chili crisp, in a small bowl, combine the chili crisp and honey and mix well. Add the grapefruit segments to the same bowl, then squeeze any juice from the remaining grapefruit core over the bowl. Gently mix, breaking up the grapefruit into smaller pieces.

To serve, drain the liquid and transfer everything to a serving bowl, then gently fold in the avocado. Place the bowl of grapefruit chili crisp next to it, with the romaine leaves and mint alongside. To eat, add a spoonful of ceviche to a lettuce leaf and top with grapefruit chili crisp and mint leaves.

Remix! If you can't find mahi-mahi, you can use salmon, shrimp, or even scallops (for shellfish, marinate 1 hour).

SLOW-ROASTED SALMON *with Five-Spice* *Brown Butter*

SERVES 4

So, here's my salmon confession: As a child I was neutral on salmon, likely due to early morning fishing trips with my dad just outside San Francisco Bay, where the violently treacherous waters under the Golden Gate Bridge would often turn me varying shades of green. The last thing I cared about was some fish flopping around on the boat deck. But that was then and this is now—and salmon is my go-to when I cook at home. Slow-roasting it is how I cook it almost all of the time, and for good reason: Cooking salmon low and slow renders the fish buttery and tender without risk of overcooking. The result is truly unctuous and becomes even more luxurious when paired with a nutty brown butter spiked with the warming notes of five-spice and the sweet zip of orange. This dish is ideal for entertaining, as the brown butter can be made ahead of time and gently reheated, and the oven does the rest of the work.

3 tablespoons unsalted butter

1 teaspoon five-spice powder

Grated zest and juice of 1 orange

1 (2- to 2½-pound) skin-on salmon fillet

Kosher salt

Freshly ground black pepper

3 or 4 radishes

¼ cup mix of roughly chopped dill, flat-leaf parsley, cilantro, and chives

Flaky sea salt, for finishing

Preheat the oven to 250°F with a rack in the center position.

In a small saucepan, melt the butter over medium heat until the foaming subsides, brown bits appear at the bottom of the saucepan, and the butter is a fragrant, nutty golden brown, about 3 minutes. Remove the pan from the heat and stir in the five-spice and orange zest and juice.

Place the salmon skin side down in a 9 × 13-inch roasting pan and season the flesh side with 2 teaspoons kosher salt and ½ teaspoon pepper. Pour the butter mixture over the salmon, using a spoon to cover it completely. Roast for 25 to 35 minutes, basting once halfway through, until the thickest part of the fillet registers 120°F.

Use a mandoline or a very sharp knife to slice the radishes into paper-thin slices.

To serve, break up the fillet into 4 large pieces and arrange on a platter. Spoon the buttery pan juices atop, garnish with the radishes and herbs, and finish with flaky sea salt.

PANKO SALMON
with Labneh Dijonnaise

SERVES 4

My go-to French spot in NYC's West Village, La Ripaille, serves a lovely salmon with dijonnaise sauce, and having eaten it so many times, I sought to create my own version. Here, I've coated the fillet tops with a crunchy panko mixture and infused the mayo with labneh for tang along with the malted saltiness of soy sauce. I love serving this for company because it's so quick—the panko and Dijonnaise can be made in advance for a stress-free evening.

1 tablespoon unsalted butter

2 teaspoons extra-virgin olive oil

1 cup panko

2 teaspoons fennel seeds

½ teaspoon five-spice powder

⅓ cup Kewpie mayonnaise

1 tablespoon white miso

Kosher salt

Freshly ground black pepper

4 (8-ounce) salmon fillets

2 tablespoons minced chives

LABNEH DIJONNAISE

½ cup labneh

3 tablespoons Kewpie mayonnaise

3 tablespoons Dijon mustard

1 teaspoon soy sauce

1 teaspoon rice wine vinegar

1 teaspoon honey

Kosher salt

Freshly ground black pepper

Preheat the oven to 425°F with a rack in the lower third of the oven. Line a rimmed baking sheet with parchment paper.

Heat the butter and oil in a large nonstick skillet over medium heat until the butter has melted. Add the panko, fennel seeds, and five-spice and cook, stirring frequently, until the panko is pale golden brown, about 5 minutes. Transfer to a shallow bowl or plate and let cool.

In a small bowl, whisk together the mayonnaise and miso. Season with ¼ teaspoon salt and ⅛ teaspoon pepper.

Place the fillets skin side down on the prepared baking sheet. Spread the mayonnaise mixture on the flesh side of each fillet, then coat the prepared tops with the panko mixture, patting the panko down so it adheres. Bake for 13 to 15 minutes for medium-rare, or until the center of the thickest fillet registers 120°F.

Meanwhile, make the Dijonnaise. In a medium bowl, whisk together the labneh, mayonnaise, Dijon, soy sauce, rice wine vinegar, and honey until smooth and creamy. Season with salt and pepper. Transfer to a small serving bowl.

To serve, arrange the salmon on a platter, garnish with the chives, and serve with the Dijonnaise alongside.

Try With Asparagus and Fennel with Gribiche-y Dressing (page 38).

Remix! If you can't find labneh, use Greek yogurt.

SHRIMP *and* LYCHEE CEVICHE

SERVES 4

When I started writing this book, I knew I had to fit lychees in it somewhere. As a kid I loved them so much I'd sneak a can down to my room and eat them in secrecy, relishing each glossy orb and the floral sweetness of the syrup before popping them into my mouth and figuring out where to dispose of the can. While I've used them in the dessert section in my Lychee Lime Pavlova (page 219), I also love how they pair up with savory dishes. Here, the heat of a jalapeño is the perfect foil for plump shrimp and the delicate burst of succulent lychees.

1 pound medium shrimp, peeled, deveined, and cut in half lengthwise

Kosher salt

10 to 12 canned lychees, cut in half, plus 2 tablespoons syrup from the can

½ cup fresh lime juice (about 5 limes), plus lime wedges for serving

½ cup fresh lemon juice (4 to 5 lemons)

1 jalapeño, seeded and thinly sliced

1 small red onion, very thinly sliced (¼ to ½ cup)

¼ cup roughly chopped cilantro leaves and tender stems, plus more leaves for garnish

2 mini cucumbers, halved lengthwise and cut into ½-inch slices

1 teaspoon maple syrup

¼ teaspoon grated fresh ginger

Put the shrimp in a large bowl, season with salt, and add the lychees and syrup, lime juice, lemon juice, jalapeño, red onion, cilantro, cucumbers, maple syrup, and ginger. Mix to combine, cover tightly, and refrigerate for about 2 hours, or until the shrimp are opaque.

Transfer the shrimp to a serving platter. Garnish with the cilantro and lime wedges and serve chilled.

Hot Tip Fresh lychees can be used. Make sure to pit them and add a splash more maple syrup as you won't have any juice from the can.

Remix! You can use precooked shrimp, but marinate for only 15 to 30 minutes.

Speedy Stir-Fry
GINGER SHRIMP

SERVES 4

This was Grandma's back-pocket recipe because it was quick, easy, and—as with all stir-fries—the sizzling-hot wok took care of all the heavy lifting. The dish is almost exactly how she would have made it, down to the meticulous drying of the shrimp by hanging them off the side of a bowl (if you must, you can also pat them dry with several paper towels). My one addition is a squeeze of lime juice at the end for an acidic kick that plays so well with the garlic and ginger. I think she'd approve.

1 pound large shrimp, peeled and deveined

1 teaspoon five-spice powder

Kosher salt

Freshly ground black pepper

1 tablespoon neutral oil

1 (1-inch) piece fresh ginger, grated

3 garlic cloves, finely minced

4 scallions, cut into 2-inch lengths

1 tablespoon soy sauce

1 tablespoon pale dry sherry

2 tablespoons fresh lime juice, plus lime wedges for serving

Cilantro leaves, for garnish (optional)

Pat the shrimp dry with a paper towel and hang them over the edge of a large bowl for 10 minutes to thoroughly dry. Transfer to the bowl and season with the five-spice, ½ teaspoon salt, and ¼ teaspoon pepper.

Heat the neutral oil in a wok or large skillet over high heat. Add the ginger and garlic. Once the ginger is sizzling, add the shrimp and sauté for 2 to 3 minutes, or until just opaque. Turn the heat up to medium-high, add the scallions, soy sauce, and sherry, and toss to coat the shrimp.

Transfer the shrimp to a serving platter, finish with the lime juice, garnish with cilantro (if using), and serve with lime wedges.

Lemony Miso
GARLIC SHRIMP

SERVES 4

A total winner of a Tuesday dinner. What takes the longest is the marinating of the shrimp—the rest happens in 5. How can you beat that?

6 garlic cloves, minced (about ¼ cup)

Grated zest and juice of 1 lemon, divided, plus lemon wedges for serving

2 tablespoons extra-virgin olive oil

1 tablespoon miso

¼ teaspoon chili flakes

Kosher salt

Freshly ground black pepper

1 pound extra jumbo (16/20) shrimp, peeled and deveined (tails left on if desired)

4 tablespoons unsalted butter, divided

2 tablespoons chopped flat-leaf parsley

2 tablespoons chopped cilantro

Steamed jasmine rice or grilled bread, for serving

In a medium bowl, combine the garlic, lemon zest, half the lemon juice, olive oil, miso, chili flakes, ¼ teaspoon salt, and ¼ teaspoon pepper. Whisk until the miso is dissolved, then add the shrimp and gently mix to coat. Let marinate for 15 minutes.

In a large cast-iron skillet or other heavy pan, melt the butter over medium heat. Add the remaining lemon juice and mix to combine, then add the shrimp in a single layer, along with the marinade.

Cook the shrimp for about 2½ minutes per side, or until opaque and cooked through and the garlic is softened. Remove the pan from the heat and stir in the parsley and cilantro.

Add the lemon wedges and serve the shrimp from the pan, with rice or grilled bread alongside.

Mix In Add a can of drained, rinsed cannellini beans for a heartier take.

Remix! Noodle-ize this dish! Toss with 1 pound cooked linguine or spaghetti, adding ½ cup or so of the pasta cooking water to the sauce and tossing with the noodles and shrimp to emulsify.

SOLE MEUNIÈRE
with Fish Sauce and Lime

SERVES 4

Much like Julia Child, my mom's love of French food started with this dish. While Julia was in Normandy in 1963, my mom, as she tells me, was in Paris (on a budget of $5 a day), wedged between two large Gauloises-puffing Frenchmen at a tiny postage stamp of a restaurant. When the plate arrived at the table, the perfume of browned butter and lemon was intoxicating (the wafting cigarette smoke notwithstanding). She tucked in and ate the entire thing (which, if you know my mom, is no surprise), elbow to elbow with her fellow diners in true Parisian fashion. Once back home, she cracked open her well-worn copy of Louis Diat's *Gourmet's Basic French Cooking* and found the recipe, and the rest is history. When I was growing up, she'd often make it for dinner, as it was fast and relatively easy, with only a few ingredients. The pan would come out and sole meunière—in all of its buttery lemony glory—would make a Tuesday feel like a special occasion. Here, I've infused the butter with fish sauce for another layer of flavor and used limes for their slightly sweet tartness.

4 (6-ounce) sole fillets

Kosher salt

Freshly ground black pepper

½ cup all-purpose flour

1 tablespoon neutral oil

5 tablespoons unsalted European-style butter, divided

¼ cup capers, drained and rinsed

1½ tablespoons fish sauce

Grated zest and juice of 1 lime (about 2 tablespoons juice), plus lime wedges for serving

¼ cup finely chopped mix of flat-leaf parsley and cilantro

Pat the fish dry on both sides with a paper towel, then season with salt and pepper. Pour the flour into a shallow bowl or plate and coat the fish evenly, shaking off any excess.

Heat the oil and 1 tablespoon of the butter in a large skillet over medium heat until the butter is melted and shimmering. Working in batches if necessary, carefully lay the fish in the pan and cook until just cooked through, about 2 minutes per side. Transfer to a serving platter.

To the pan, add the remaining 4 tablespoons butter and the capers and melt the butter, whisking frequently, until it turns a nutty golden brown, 4 to 5 minutes. Whisk in the fish sauce and lime zest and juice. Pour the butter mixture over the fillets, garnish with the herbs, add lime wedges to the platter, and serve immediately.

One Big
SEAFOOD POT PIE

SERVES 4 TO 6

This dish is a playful riff on Mom's signature go-to for fancy dinner parties: shrimp in Mornay sauce served in little Pepperidge Farm puff pastry shells (also known as vol-au-vents if we're getting fancy)—a gem straight from her note card from Friday, April 14, 1972, but now supersized and a true family style feast. The title says it all: a generous pan of shrimp and fish in a dreamy, creamy sauce, finished with a crown of puff pastry that's baked separately in the same oven, then placed atop when ready to serve.

¼ cup all-purpose flour, plus more for dusting

2 sheets frozen puff pastry, thawed

1 large egg beaten with 1 tablespoon water

8 tablespoons (1 stick) unsalted butter

1 large onion, minced

2 leeks, white and light green parts only, sliced

4 garlic cloves, sliced

2 tablespoons thyme leaves

2 bay leaves

Kosher salt

Freshly ground black pepper

¼ cup dry white wine, such as Sauvignon Blanc or Chardonnay

2 cups fish or seafood stock

1 tablespoon fish sauce

¼ cup heavy cream

1 pound large shrimp, peeled, deveined, and cut in half lengthwise

1 pound firm white fish, such as cod or halibut, cut into large, bite-size pieces

1 cup frozen peas

1 cup frozen pearl onions

½ cup chopped flat-leaf parsley

1 teaspoon flaky sea salt

Preheat the oven to 375°F with racks in the upper and lower thirds of the oven. Line a rimmed baking sheet with parchment paper.

Lightly dust the countertop with flour and use a rolling pin to roll out each puff pastry sheet to about a 13-inch square. Transfer one pastry sheet to the prepared baking sheet. Brush with some of the egg wash, then place the second pastry sheet directly on top. Working quickly, use your hands to press on both sheets so they adhere. Place the baking sheet in the fridge.

In a 12-inch cast-iron skillet or other heavy pan, melt the butter over medium heat. Add the onion, leeks, garlic, thyme, and bay leaves, season with kosher salt and pepper, and sauté until softened, about 7 minutes.

(recipe continues)

Turn the heat down to medium-low and add the flour. Mix to coat and let the mixture toast for 1 minute. Add the wine and simmer for 3 minutes, then add the fish stock and fish sauce and cook, stirring, until the mixture has thickened, 3 to 4 minutes. Season again with kosher salt and pepper, then stir in the cream. Remove and discard the bay leaves. Add the shrimp, fish, peas, pearl onions, and parsley and gently mix to combine.

Remove the puff pastry from the fridge and cut it into a 12-inch circle using a lid or a plate as a guide. Brush with the remaining egg wash and sprinkle with flaky sea salt.

Place the skillet with the seafood mixture on the lower oven rack. Place the baking sheet with the puff pastry on the upper rack. Bake for 25 minutes, then remove the fish and continue to bake the puff pastry for 10 more minutes, or until it is puffed and golden brown.

Carefully place the puff pastry directly atop the seafood mixture and serve immediately.

SUMMER ROLL FISH TACOS
with Spicy Peanut Sauce

SERVES 4
(8 TACOS)

The flavors of Vietnamese summer rolls—along with their accompanying peanut dipping sauce—and tacos combine for a delicious summery bite.

FISH

2 teaspoons ground coriander

2 teaspoons ground ginger

2 teaspoons garlic powder

½ teaspoon chili powder

Kosher salt

Freshly ground black pepper

4 (6-ounce) firm white fish fillets, such as cod, hake, or halibut

1 tablespoon extra-virgin olive oil

SPICY PEANUT SAUCE

¼ cup smooth peanut butter

¼ cup canned unsweetened coconut cream

3 tablespoons fresh lime juice

1 tablespoon chili crisp, or more to taste

2 teaspoons soy sauce

2 teaspoons brown sugar

2 teaspoons fish sauce

Kosher salt

TACO FIXINGS

1 tablespoon neutral oil

8 small soft corn tortillas

1 head romaine lettuce

1 cup shredded carrots

¼ cup roughly chopped roasted peanuts

Mint, cilantro, and basil leaves, for garnish

Lime wedges, for serving

Preheat the oven to 375°F. Line a rimmed baking sheet with aluminum foil.

In a small bowl, mix the coriander, ginger, garlic powder, chili powder, 1 teaspoon salt, and ½ teaspoon pepper. Rub each fish fillet with olive oil, then coat with the spice mix. Transfer to the prepared baking sheet and roast for 20 to 25 minutes, or until the fish is tender and flaky.

While the fish is baking, make the spicy peanut sauce. In a bowl, whisk together the peanut butter, coconut cream, lime juice, chili crisp, soy sauce, brown sugar, fish sauce, and ½ teaspoon salt until smooth.

In a large cast-iron skillet or other heavy pan, heat the neutral oil over high heat. Working in batches, heat the tortillas until soft and just browned on the edges, 1 to 2 minutes per side. Transfer to a plate and cover with a kitchen towel. *(recipe continues)*

To assemble each taco, tear half a leaf of romaine and place on a tortilla (the rib of the romaine is where the tortilla will fold), add a portion of fish, then top with some carrots. Add a dollop of the peanut sauce, then garnish with peanuts and herbs. Serve on a platter with lime wedges and the remaining peanut sauce alongside.

Hot Tip Use 5-inch soft corn tortillas or bigger; any smaller and the filling will spill out.

TUNA *with Roasted Cherry and Caper Salsa*

SERVES 4

Sometimes, crafting a dish is like telling a well-timed bon mot—it should be effortlessly amusing and leave one wanting more. And well, frankly my dears, that's what this cherry and caper salsa does. The ping-pong of briny capers and succulent cherries is quite the witty repartee to stand up perfectly to tuna's meaty tender texture—and will leave you definitely wanting more.

⅓ cup very thinly sliced red onion

¼ cup sherry vinegar

Kosher salt

2 tablespoons capers, drained and rinsed

1 teaspoon grated lime zest

2 tablespoons fresh lime juice

1 tablespoon extra-virgin olive oil, plus more for finishing

½ teaspoon oyster sauce

¼ cup roughly chopped cilantro leaves and tender stems, plus more for garnish (optional)

1 jalapeño, seeded and finely minced

½ teaspoon brown sugar

Freshly ground black pepper

4 (8-ounce) tuna steaks (about 1 inch thick)

1 tablespoon neutral oil

1½ cups pitted fresh cherries (about 8 ounces)

Put the onion in a small bowl and toss with the sherry vinegar, ¼ cup water, and a pinch of salt. Let sit for 20 to 30 minutes, tossing occasionally, until softened.

In a medium bowl, combine the capers, lime zest and juice, olive oil, oyster sauce, cilantro, jalapeño, and brown sugar. Season with salt and pepper and mix to combine; set aside.

Season the tuna generously with salt and pepper. Place a large cast-iron skillet or other heavy pan over high heat. When the pan is very hot, add the neutral oil, then add the tuna steaks, in batches if necessary. Cook for 1½ minutes per side, or until just cooked through but still rare in the center. Transfer to a plate.

Add the cherries to the same pan, turn the heat down to medium, and cook, stirring only once or twice and using the back of a wooden spoon to crush some of them, for 2 to 3 minutes, or until they start to char in spots and break down. Transfer to the bowl with the caper mixture and toss to combine. Add the red onion to the bowl, along with 1 tablespoon of the pickling liquid.

Slice the tuna and arrange on a platter, then top with the salsa. Finish with a glug of olive oil, garnish with cilantro (if using), and serve.

Try With Radicchio and Fennel Salad with Creamy Miso Maple Dressing (page 46).

Remix! Use frozen cherries—thawed—if fresh aren't available.

Another Remix! Try the salsa with pork chops, roasted brussels sprouts, or chicken.

POACHED CHICKEN
with Two Dips

SERVES 4

Grandma was a pharmacist, which was quite rare for Hong Kong in the 1920s. But that training meant that she was very precise with her measurements—experimenting with proportions and ingredients until she got things right. My auntie Gloria recalls that in the 1950s she and Grandpa (himself quite the gourmand) drove three or four times from San Francisco to Mountain View (which back then would be a 2-hour car ride) because there was a restaurant that had a good version of saltwater chicken and she wanted to imitate the recipe correctly. Based on my grandma's well-researched recipe—and Cantonese classic bak jit quy (which translates to "white cut chicken")—my quick take eschews boiling the entire chicken and sticks to the breasts to cut down significantly on cooking time. And while the traditional version boils the chicken in water, I've used chicken stock to impart even more flavor. Serving the chicken with two dips is the customary way to do it, and besides the addition of chili crisp to the soy version, these are exactly how Grandma, and later Mom, have made them for decades.

4 boneless, skinless chicken breasts (about 1½ to 2 pounds)

6 cups low-sodium chicken stock

2 star anise

2 bay leaves

1 teaspoon neutral oil (optional)

Sliced scallions and cilantro leaves, for garnish

HERBY GINGER SAUCE

⅓ cup neutral oil

2 tablespoons toasted sesame oil

2 teaspoons finely grated fresh ginger

2 scallions, thinly sliced, plus more for garnish

2 tablespoons finely chopped cilantro leaves and tender stems, plus more for garnish

Kosher salt

SPICY SOY SAUCE

⅓ cup soy sauce

1 teaspoon chili oil

1 teaspoon chili crisp

1 teaspoon toasted sesame oil

1 teaspoon mirin

Combine the chicken breasts, chicken stock, star anise, and bay leaves in a large pot or Dutch oven. Add more stock (or water) as needed to ensure the chicken is submerged.

Turn the heat to medium. When the liquid just starts to simmer, turn the heat down to low to maintain a very low simmer. Cover and cook for 10 minutes, then turn off the heat and let sit, covered, for another 10 minutes, or until the

(recipe continues)

internal temperature of the chicken is 155°F. Remove the chicken from the liquid and let cool, then wrap the chicken and place in the fridge to chill for at least 1 hour.

When ready to serve, make the sauces. For the herby ginger sauce, in a small bowl, mix the neutral oil, sesame oil, ginger, scallions, cilantro, and ½ teaspoon salt. For the spicy soy sauce, in a second small bowl, mix the soy sauce, chili oil, chili crisp, sesame oil, mirin, and 1½ tablespoons water.

To serve, rub the chicken with the neutral oil (this is purely for aesthetic reasons, so you can skip it if you like), then cut the chicken into ½-inch-thick slices. Arrange on a platter and garnish with the scallions and cilantro. Serve the sauces alongside for dipping.

Hot Tip Bak jit quy is traditionally a cold dish, so I've indicated to chill the cooked chicken, but it is also delicious warm if you're short on time.

Grandma and Grandpa in Vancouver, late 1960s.

Mike's CHINESE CHICKEN SALAD

SERVES 4 TO 6

Who is Mike? And why do I love his chicken salad? Mike's Chinese Cuisine on Geary Street in San Francisco, owned by the affable Mike Won and his wife, Lily, was the family's de facto gathering spot for dinner out when I was growing up—whether a table for 6 or for full-on banquets that took over the entire restaurant, like we did for Grandma's 90th birthday. Our family went there so often that my parents did the interior redesign of the space. But no matter how many people or how many courses, one constant prevailed: Chinese chicken salad.

Mike's version eschewed the usual mall food court fallbacks that one sees—nary a crispy noodle, cashew, or mandarin orange segment (or even soy sauce!) here. Instead, his version was based on sau sie guy—which literally translates to "hand-torn chicken." So yes, using one's impeccably clean hands to tear the chicken is key, but the other key is to make sure that the lettuce is similarly shredded and that the scallions are julienned. This dish is the perfect main for a lunch or light summer dinner, along with some herbed farro or grilled vegetables.

1 teaspoon neutral oil

2 boneless, skinless chicken breasts (about 1 to 1½ pounds)

Kosher salt

Freshly ground black pepper

1 small head iceberg lettuce, finely shredded

3 scallions, julienned, plus more for garnish

½ cup cilantro leaves and tender stems, plus more for garnish

¼ cup roughly chopped roasted peanuts, plus more for garnish

DRESSING

3½ tablespoons neutral oil

2 tablespoons lemon juice

1½ tablespoons toasted sesame oil

1½ tablespoons rice wine vinegar

1½ tablespoons Dijon mustard

1 teaspoon sugar

½ teaspoon five-spice powder

Kosher salt

½ teaspoon ground white pepper

Preheat the oven to 425°F with a rack in the center position. Line a rimmed baking sheet with parchment paper.

Rub the neutral oil on the chicken breasts and season with salt and pepper. Put them on the prepared baking sheet and roast for 25 to 30 minutes, or until the internal temperature registers 165°F. Set aside to cool for 10 to 15 minutes, then use your impeccably clean hands or two forks to tear into bite-size julienned pieces. *(recipe continues)*

To make the dressing, in a large bowl, whisk together the neutral oil, lemon juice, sesame oil, rice wine vinegar, Dijon mustard, sugar, five-spice, 2 teaspoons salt, and white pepper.

Add the chicken to the dressing and toss to coat thoroughly, then add the iceberg, scallions, cilantro, and peanuts and gently toss to combine.

Mound the chicken salad onto a platter, garnish with additional cilantro, scallions, and peanuts, and serve.

Remix! My auntie Gloria often uses Little Gem lettuce instead of iceberg for a fancier take (it also holds up better once dressed).

Grandma, all smiles, for her 90th birthday at Mike's, 1996.

Mom's
FIVE-SPICE CHICKEN
(But on a Sheet Pan)

SERVES 4

Spice up your life! But really fast. Mom's famous five-spice chicken was on the menu weekly when I was growing up and eventually became the dish that reignited my interest in cooking. While Mom roasted the whole bird to delicious and, frankly, legendary effect, I've sped things up by roasting thighs and drumsticks on a sheet pan along with bok choy. It's a super simple weeknight sheet pan version that still has tender juicy chicken with that crispy, crunchy skin flecked with five-spice.

1 tablespoon five-spice powder

Kosher salt

Freshly ground black pepper

1 teaspoon sugar

1 teaspoon baking powder

4 each bone-in, skin-on chicken thighs and drumsticks (about 3 pounds)

3 teaspoons neutral oil, divided

1 small red onion, cut into ½-inch wedges

4 scallions, trimmed, plus 1 scallion, sliced, for garnish

1 pound baby bok choy, halved lengthwise

Cilantro leaves and tender stems, for garnish

Steamed jasmine rice, for serving

Chili crisp, for serving

Preheat the oven to 450°F with a rack in the center position. Line a rimmed baking sheet with parchment paper.

In a small skillet, toast the five-spice, 1 tablespoon salt, and 1 teaspoon pepper over medium-low heat until fragrant, 1 to 2 minutes. Transfer to a small bowl and let cool for 5 minutes, then stir in the sugar and baking powder.

Pat the chicken dry with a paper towel and rub with 2 teaspoons of the oil. Season the chicken on all sides with the five-spice mixture and arrange skin side up on the prepared baking sheet, along with the sliced onion and whole scallions. Roast for 15 minutes.

Remove the baking sheet from the oven and use tongs to arrange the bok choy among the chicken. Drizzle the bok choy with the remaining 1 teaspoon oil and season with salt and pepper.

Return to the oven and roast for another 10 minutes, or until the vegetables start to soften and get some color. If desired, turn the broiler on high to crisp up the chicken skin for 2 to 3 minutes. Garnish with cilantro and sliced scallion. Serve the chicken and cooking juices over steamed jasmine rice, with chili crisp on the side.

CHICKEN THIGHS
with Cherry Tomatoes and Spicy Anchovy Breadcrumbs

SERVES 4

Cherry tomatoes play a big role in my cooking as they're always available and ready to use, and they bring acid and sweet brightness to any dish. They're the perfect complement to chicken thighs—so succulent and meaty and forgiving to cook. Frankly, this dish couldn't be easier, so while I'd call it a Tuesday kind of meal, it's really an every day of the week kind of meal.

1 small fennel bulb

2 pints cherry tomatoes

3 garlic cloves, sliced

1 tablespoon extra-virgin olive oil

2 teaspoons honey

2 teaspoons balsamic vinegar

1 teaspoon mustard powder

1 teaspoon ground coriander, divided

10 thyme sprigs, plus more for garnish

4 to 6 bone-in, skin-on chicken thighs (about 2 to 2½ pounds)

Kosher salt

Freshly ground black pepper

ANCHOVY BREADCRUMBS

1 tablespoon extra-virgin olive oil, plus more for finishing

1 tablespoon anchovy paste

½ cup panko

1 teaspoon togarashi

Kosher salt

Freshly ground black pepper

Flaky sea salt, for finishing

Preheat the oven to 425°F. Line a rimmed baking sheet or roasting pan with parchment paper.

Core the fennel and use a mandoline or very sharp knife to slice into paper-thin slices. Reserve the fronds for garnish.

Put the fennel, cherry tomatoes, and garlic on the prepared baking sheet. Add the olive oil, honey, balsamic, mustard powder, and ½ teaspoon of the coriander and toss to coat thoroughly. Add the thyme sprigs. Pat the chicken dry on all sides with a paper towel and season well with kosher salt, pepper, and the remaining ½ teaspoon coriander. Arrange the chicken skin side up among the cherry tomatoes. Bake for 35 to 40 minutes, or until the chicken thigh skins are golden brown and crispy and the internal temperature reads 160°F.

Meanwhile, make the breadcrumbs. In a small skillet, heat the olive oil over medium heat. Add the anchovy paste and use a wooden spoon to dissolve the paste, then add the panko and togarashi. Season with salt and pepper and cook until the panko is golden brown, stirring frequently, 3 to 4 minutes.

Arrange the tomatoes and chicken on a platter and spoon some of the juices atop. Top the chicken with a bit of the panko mixture, and pour the remaining panko into a small bowl to serve alongside. Garnish the chicken with the reserved fennel fronds, finish with flaky sea salt and a glug of olive oil, and serve.

CHICKEN THIGHS
with Miso Romesco and Shallots

SERVES 4

I guess I'm a thigh man? Thighs are my go-to for most weeknight chicken dinners as they are always full of flavor and not as finicky as breasts in terms of cook time, so your risk of dry thighs is pretty much nil. But the star here is the sauce—a very versatile, luscious romesco infused with the umami of miso. It's great on chicken, but also wonderful with roasted vegetables or as a sandwich spread.

8 bone-in, skin-on chicken thighs

½ teaspoon garlic powder

Kosher salt

Freshly ground black pepper

1 tablespoon extra-virgin olive oil

5 or 6 shallots, trimmed, peeled, and halved or quartered if large

1 lemon, cut in half

3 tablespoons roughly chopped roasted almonds

Flat-leaf parsley, for garnish

Flaky sea salt, for finishing

MISO ROMESCO

1 (16-ounce) jar roasted red peppers, drained

⅓ cup roasted almonds

⅓ cup sun-dried tomatoes

1 garlic clove, peeled

2 tablespoons yellow miso

2 tablespoons rice wine vinegar

Juice of 1 lemon

1 teaspoon smoked paprika

½ teaspoon chili flakes

½ cup extra-virgin olive oil

Kosher salt

Freshly ground black pepper

Preheat the oven to 400°F with a rack in the center position.

Pat the chicken thighs dry with a paper towel, then season well with the garlic powder, kosher salt, and pepper. In a large cast-iron skillet or other ovenproof pan large enough to hold all the thighs in a single layer, heat the olive oil over medium-high heat. Add the chicken thighs skin side down and sear for 6 to 7 minutes, until the skin is golden brown. Turn the chicken over, then add the shallots and lemon halves, cut sides down, ensuring you don't cover the chicken. Transfer the pan to the oven and roast for 20 to 25 minutes, or until the internal temperature of the chicken is 165°F. Remove from the oven and let rest 10 minutes.

Meanwhile, make the romesco sauce. Combine the red peppers, almonds, sun-dried tomatoes, garlic, miso, rice wine vinegar, lemon juice, paprika, and chili flakes in a food processor. Turn the motor on and slowly stream in the olive oil until the sauce is smooth but still has some texture. Season with kosher salt and pepper and spoon into a serving bowl. (The romesco sauce can be made up to 4 days in advance and stored in an airtight container in the refrigerator.)

Garnish the chicken with the almonds, parsley, and roasted lemons (for squeezing) and finish with flaky sea salt. Serve with the romesco sauce alongside.

Try With Charred Carrots with Gochujang Honey Butter (page 72).

Famous
LEMON CHICKEN

SERVES 4 TO 6

This recipe is based on my grandma's favorite and often-made lemon chicken. My mom tells me that Grandma tested her recipe for weeks. Each time, she would tweak the recipe a bit and together Grandma and Grandpa would eat the dish and brainstorm. More lemon? Maybe a thicker sauce? I imagine Grandma and Grandpa in their dining room on Funston Avenue in San Francisco taking bites of this dish, carefully considering each and every component. In fact, Mom recalls the family eating lemon chicken for five nights straight when Grandma was working on it. So, no surprise it's since become a family staple that's been passed down. The original recipe calls for the whole bird, but I've adjusted it to chicken thighs, which cuts down on cooking time, and I've amped up the pucker-factor with double the lemon. The result is a satisfying yet light dish—the sauce is zingy, a touch sweet and a touch sour, and the lemon slices are cooked down and tender and so utterly delicious. Serve with steamed jasmine rice to soak up all that sauce.

8 bone-in, skin-on chicken thighs (about 3 pounds)

Kosher salt

Freshly ground black pepper

3 lemons

1 tablespoon neutral oil

3 scallions, thinly sliced, plus more for garnish

1 (1-inch) piece ginger, thinly sliced

¾ cup honey

¼ cup soy sauce

2 tablespoons Shaoxing wine

2½ teaspoons cornstarch

Preheat the oven to 450°F.

Pat the chicken thighs dry with a paper towel and season generously with salt and pepper. Set aside.

Use a vegetable peeler to peel 1 lemon and reserve. Juice that lemon, plus a second lemon (you should have about ½ cup). Thinly slice the third lemon and set aside.

In a large cast-iron skillet or other ovenproof pan large enough to fit the thighs in a single layer, heat the oil over medium heat until shimmering. Add the scallions, ginger, and reserved lemon peel and sauté until the scallions and lemon peel start to turn deep brown on the edges and the ginger is fragrant, 2 to 3 minutes.

Add the lemon juice, honey, soy sauce, Shaoxing wine, and 1 cup water. Season with salt and pepper, stir to combine, and let simmer for 1 to 2 minutes. Add the lemon slices, then place the chicken thighs skin side up in the pan. Transfer to the oven and roast for 35 minutes, or until the chicken skin is golden brown and the internal temperature is 165°F.

In a small bowl, stir together the cornstarch and 1½ tablespoons water. Remove the pan from the oven and use tongs to transfer the chicken

(recipe continues)

thighs to a serving platter with sides. Use a spoon to skim the fat off the surface of the pan juices. Place the pan over medium-low heat, add the cornstarch mixture, and cook, stirring occasionally, until the sauce is thickened and glossy, about 2 minutes.

Transfer some of the sauce and the lemon slices to the platter, making sure to spoon some sauce on top. Garnish with additional scallions and serve.

Try With Crispy Upside-Down Fried Rice (page 85).

Remix! Use chicken breasts instead of thighs! Roast for 18 to 25 minutes for boneless, skinless or 30 to 35 for bone-in, skin on (or until the internal temperature reads 165°F).

Hoisin HONEY ROAST CHICKEN

SERVES 4

This dish was inspired by legendary San Francisco restaurant Zuni Café's famous roast chicken, which sits atop toasted bread and is topped with a crown of greens. Here I've glazed the bird in a sweet-savory blend of orange juice, hoisin, and honey. And of course the dish wouldn't be complete without the chicken sitting atop a bed of schmaltzy, crunchy bread and finished with a generous shower of flat-leaf parsley.

1 (3½-pound) chicken, giblets removed

Kosher salt

Freshly ground black pepper

¼ cup hoisin

3 tablespoons honey

2 tablespoons orange juice

2 tablespoons neutral oil

2 teaspoons toasted sesame oil

3 garlic cloves, finely minced

2 scallions, cut into 2-inch pieces, plus thinly sliced scallions for garnish

½ cup flat-leaf parsley leaves and tender stems, plus more for garnish

2 tablespoons unsalted butter

2 or 3 (1-inch-thick) slices country bread, torn into bite-size pieces

2 tablespoons furikake

Cut the chicken under the breast from the cavity to the tail on each side, leaving a hinge. Open it up like a suitcase and place skin side up. Use the palm of your hand to flatten, especially at the breastbone.

Pat the chicken dry with a paper towel, then season generously with salt and pepper. In a large zip-top bag, combine the hoisin, honey, orange juice, neutral oil, sesame oil, garlic, scallions, parsley, a generous pinch of salt, and 4 or 5 grinds of pepper, then add the chicken. Push as much air out of the bag as possible and seal. Use your hands to massage things around so the chicken is coated in the marinade. Place the bag on a plate and refrigerate for at least 1 hour or up to 24 hours, turning the bag every few hours so the marinade coats all of the chicken.

Remove the chicken from the fridge and let it come to room temperature (30 to 45 minutes).

Preheat the oven to 400°F. Line a rimmed baking sheet with aluminum foil.

Remove the chicken from the bag, letting as much of the marinade drip back into the bag as possible, and transfer skin side up to the prepared baking sheet. Pour the marinade from the bag into a small bowl. Cover the baking sheet with foil and roast for 45 minutes. Remove the foil, baste generously with half the reserved marinade, and roast for 10 minutes, uncovered. Baste again (you should have used up all the marinade) and roast for another 10 minutes, or until the internal temperature is 165°F in the thickest part of the thigh and the chicken is burnished and deep brown.

Remove from the oven and let rest for 15 minutes, then carve.

(recipe continues)

While the chicken is resting, melt the butter in a large skillet over medium heat. Toast the bread on both sides until golden brown, about 3 minutes per side.

Put the bread on a platter and spoon the pan juices generously atop. Arrange the chicken on top. Sprinkle generously with the furikake, then garnish with sliced scallions and additional flat-leaf parsley and serve.

Try With Green Beans with Pickled Things (page 68)—put them on the bottom rack for the last 20 minutes of roasting the chicken.

Remix! You can use maple syrup if you don't have honey.

TURKEY MEATBALLS
with Corn, Stone Fruit, and Sumac Labneh

SERVES 4

This dish screams late summer and is indeed ideal to make when the market is bursting with all that August produce. It couldn't be easier: I've added sweet Italian sausage to the meatballs for instant flavor, and into the oven everything goes. Sumac—a versatile spice used in Middle Eastern cooking—lends a citrus tang with a touch of sweetness.

MEATBALLS

1 pound ground turkey

1 (4-ounce) sweet Italian sausage link, casing removed

1 large egg

⅓ cup freshly grated Pecorino Romano

⅓ cup panko

2 tablespoons chopped mint

2 tablespoons chopped flat-leaf parsley

1 teaspoon five-spice powder

¼ teaspoon cayenne pepper

Kosher salt

Freshly ground black pepper

EVERYTHING ELSE

4 ears corn, shucked and kernels cut from the cobs (2½ to 3 cups)

2 tablespoons extra-virgin olive oil, divided, plus more for finishing

Kosher salt

Freshly ground black pepper

1 cup labneh

1 ripe but firm peach, pitted and thinly sliced

1 plum, pitted and thinly sliced

2 teaspoons grated lime zest

2 teaspoons fresh lime juice

1 teaspoon ground sumac

Mint leaves, for garnish

Flaky sea salt, for finishing

Grilled country bread, for serving

Preheat the oven to 425°F.

In a large bowl, combine the ground turkey, sausage, egg, Pecorino Romano, panko, mint, parsley, five-spice, cayenne, 1½ teaspoons kosher salt, and ½ teaspoon black pepper. Use your very clean hands to combine until well mixed. Add ⅓ cup cold water and mix until the water has been absorbed. Place in the fridge to chill.

Put the corn in a 9 × 13-inch baking dish, add 1 tablespoon of the olive oil, season with ½ teaspoon kosher salt and ¼ teaspoon black pepper, and mix to combine. Spread into a single layer. Roast for 15 minutes, or until the corn is softened and starting to brown around the edges.

Remove the meatball mix from the fridge and form 16 (1½-inch) meatballs—wet your hands if needed to prevent sticking. Place the meatballs in a single layer atop the corn and return to the oven. Bake for 13 to 15 minutes, or until the internal temperature of the meatballs is 165°F.

Meanwhile, in a small bowl, mix the labneh with the remaining 1 tablespoon olive oil, season with kosher salt and black pepper, and set aside.

Remove the baking dish from the oven and arrange the peach and plum slices around the meatballs. Add dollops of the labneh, then sprinkle with the lime zest and juice and the sumac. Drizzle with a glug of olive oil, garnish with mint leaves, and finish with flaky sea salt. Serve warm with grilled bread alongside.

Hot Tip These meatballs are perfect with my Parm Wonton Broth (page 31).

Remix! Don't have fresh corn? Use frozen. Don't eat pork? Use Italian chicken sausage instead.

CORNISH GAME HENS
with Garlicky Mushroom Rice

SERVES 4

When I was growing up, Mom would make Cornish game hens for special-occasion fancy-ish dinners, and I can understand why. Each person got their own bird (or half, if they were large), eliminating any squabble over light and dark meat, and the stuffing—usually wild rice and mushroom—was flavored by being stuffed inside the cavity. Plus, no last-minute bird carving—everyone does that on their own. Cornish game hens, a smaller and more tender breed, might not always be on display at your local butcher's, so a polite request to pull them from the back or order them ahead might be necessary. However, the effort is well rewarded. Here, I've halved the hens and cooked them on a bed of tender fluffy rice studded with mushrooms—and it all happens in one pan.

1 cup jasmine rice

2 (14- to 16-ounce) Cornish game hens

3 tablespoons neutral oil, divided

1½ tablespoons hoisin sauce, divided

1 tablespoon maple syrup

1 teaspoon ground coriander

Kosher salt

Freshly ground black pepper

2 shallots, minced

5 garlic cloves, minced

2 scallions, thinly sliced

8 ounces button mushrooms, cut into bite-size pieces

¼ cup minced cilantro, plus more leaves for garnish

1½ cups chicken stock

2 tablespoons unsalted butter, cubed

Try With Cauliflower Marbella (page 64).

Preheat the oven to 375°F.

Rinse the jasmine rice in a large bowl 2 or 3 times, changing the water each time and using your impeccably clean hands to agitate the rice until the water runs almost clear, then drain. Set aside.

Use kitchen shears or a sharp knife to cut each hen in half lengthwise through the breastbone to cut in half completely, then transfer to a rimmed baking sheet, skin side up, and pat dry with a paper towel.

In a small bowl, whisk together 1 tablespoon of the oil, 1 tablespoon of the hoisin, the maple syrup, and the coriander and brush the mixture on the hens. Season with salt and pepper.

In a 12-inch cast-iron skillet, heat the remaining 2 tablespoons oil over medium heat. Add the shallots, garlic, and scallions and sauté until softened, about 2 minutes. Add the mushrooms, rice, and cilantro, season with salt and pepper, and mix to combine. Add the chicken stock and remaining ½ tablespoon hoisin and stir to combine, then bring to a simmer.

Remove the pan from the heat, dot the rice with the butter cubes, then place the hens skin side up on top of the rice. Cover the pan with aluminum foil, transfer to the oven, and roast for 30 minutes, then remove the foil and roast for another 15 minutes, or until the skin is golden brown and the internal temperature registers 165°F. Garnish with additional cilantro and serve.

Kinda Fancy
ORANGE DUCK CONFIT

SERVES 4

Don't fear duck. It is often seen as chichi and hard to prepare, but this recipe is actually quite simple to make, though it feels elegant. My friend Claire is duck-obsessed and urgently requests this dish every time she comes over for dinner—so who am I to deny her? Really, it's a win-win for everyone. Orange and duck are a match made in French culinary heaven, so I'm not messing with a good thing. In this case I've made that good thing even easier—with only a handful of ingredients and letting the oven do virtually all of the work.

1 tablespoon five-spice powder

2 teaspoons sugar

Kosher salt

Freshly ground black pepper

4 Moulard duck legs

½ small head cabbage, cut into ½-inch slices

6 thyme sprigs

3 tablespoons orange marmalade

1 tablespoon fresh lemon juice, plus more for finishing

Thinly sliced orange peel or grated orange zest, for garnish

Cilantro leaves and tender stems, for garnish (optional)

Flaky sea salt, for finishing

In a small bowl, mix the five-spice, sugar, 1 tablespoon kosher salt, and 2 teaspoons pepper.

Dry the duck legs with a paper towel, then prick the skin with the tip of a knife (don't pierce the flesh). Rub the legs generously all over with spice mixture, then cover and let sit for 1 hour at room temperature (or up to 24 hours in the fridge).

Arrange the cabbage slices in a single layer in a 9 × 13-inch baking dish, add the thyme, then place the duck legs in a single layer atop. Cover tightly with aluminum foil. Place in the cold oven, turn the oven temperature to 300°F, and bake for 2 hours. Do not preheat the oven! This is an important step—the gentle warming of the oven will render out the fat.

When the duck is just about done, combine the marmalade and lemon juice in a small saucepan and simmer over low heat until just thinned out, about 2 minutes.

Remove the duck from the oven and turn the broiler on low. Remove the foil and brush the marmalade liberally on the duck and cabbage. Return to the oven and broil for 5 minutes, or until the skin is crisp.

Transfer the duck to a platter and spoon some of the duck fat atop. Garnish with orange peel or zest and cilantro (if using). Finish with a squeeze of lemon juice and flaky sea salt and serve.

Try With Radicchio and Fennel Salad with Creamy Miso Maple Dressing (page 46).

Hot Tip Speaking of duck fat: Save it! Duck fat is liquid gold with a rich flavor and perfect for roasting potatoes and vegetables. Store it in an airtight container in the fridge for up to 6 months.

STIR-FRIED BEEF
with Onions 'n' Shrooms

SERVES 4

Stir-fries are the little black dress of Chinese cooking: super versatile and able to be accessorized and changed up in any which way. This recipe, a staple in my mom's weeknight arsenal, is a speedy affair, bursting with pantry-staple flavor bombs she always keeps at the ready. As with all stir-fries, there are two rules. First, the higher the heat, the closer to *yum*. That's right, high heat rules, so you'll want to skip the nonstick pan (which typically is recommended only for low to medium heat) and grab a sturdy wok or cast-iron or stainless steel skillet. Second, chop and prep everything in advance. When using such high heat, cooking happens very quickly—like, within seconds—so you'll need your ingredients chopped and ready to go.

5 tablespoons neutral oil, divided

2 tablespoons soy sauce

1 tablespoon oyster sauce

1 tablespoon pale dry sherry

½ teaspoon sugar

3 teaspoons cornstarch, divided

Kosher salt

Freshly ground black pepper

1 pound flank steak, thinly sliced across the grain

1 (1-inch) piece ginger, julienned

3 garlic cloves, minced

1 medium white onion, thinly sliced

3 scallions, thinly sliced, white and green parts separated

1 pound shiitake mushrooms, stemmed and halved if large

1½ teaspoons toasted sesame oil

1 tablespoon grated orange zest

1 cup basil leaves, divided

Steamed jasmine rice, for serving

Mix 3 tablespoons of the neutral oil, the soy sauce, oyster sauce, sherry, sugar, 1 teaspoon of the cornstarch, ½ teaspoon salt, and ¼ teaspoon pepper in a medium bowl. Add the beef, toss to coat, and let marinate for 10 to 15 minutes.

In a small bowl, whisk together the remaining 2 teaspoons cornstarch with 3 tablespoons water until fully dissolved. Set aside.

In a wok or large, heavy skillet, heat the remaining 2 tablespoons neutral oil over high heat. Add the beef, spread out into a single layer, and let cook undisturbed for 45 seconds, or until browned, then stir for 15 seconds. Transfer to a plate.

Add the ginger, garlic, onion, and scallion whites and sauté until the onion is just translucent, 3 to 4 minutes. Add the mushrooms and sauté for 3 to 4 minutes, or until the mushrooms are tender. Add the cornstarch mixture and stir for 30 to 45 seconds, or until the sauce has thickened. Return the beef (and any juices from the plate) to the wok and stir to combine for 15 to 20 seconds.

Remove the wok from the heat and stir in the sesame oil, orange zest, and half the basil leaves. Season with salt and pepper. Transfer to a platter, garnish with the scallion greens and remaining basil, and serve immediately, with jasmine rice alongside.

Remix! This is just as delish without the beef! Just double up on the mushrooms and mix up the varieties you use.

Big Beautiful BEEF STEW

SERVES 4 TO 6

Besides my Mom's Five-Spice Chicken (page 146), beef stew was one of the first things I learned to cook upon moving to New York. It's a very forgiving dish for a beginner 'cause the oven does most of the work. And boy did I work it—my early dinner parties in those days in my tiny Kips Bay shabby-chic (more shabby, not so chic) apartment most often consisted of a few work friends, my roommate, and whatever guy I currently had a crush on. Around the table we'd listen to Pet Shop Boys and Black Box and feast on beef stew, a salad, hunks of French bread (and about 15 bottles of cheap Chianti). I've infused some of my favorite Asian pantry staples into this recipe for a deep, rich, intense flavor. Serve with steamed jasmine rice, polenta, or mashed potatoes—or thick slices of country bread to soak up all that sauce.

1½ cups dry red wine

½ cup soy sauce

¼ cup hoisin sauce

4 tablespoons extra-virgin olive oil, divided, plus more as needed

2 tablespoons honey

2 tablespoons sriracha

1 tablespoon white miso

Freshly ground black pepper

3 pounds boneless beef chuck, cut into 1½-inch pieces

¼ cup all-purpose flour

Kosher salt

1 large yellow onion, cut into 1-inch pieces

4 medium carrots, cut into 1-inch pieces

8 garlic cloves, peeled and smashed

2 cups low-sodium beef stock

2 bay leaves

1½ cups frozen peas

¼ cup chopped flat-leaf parsley

In a medium bowl, combine the wine, soy sauce, hoisin, 2 tablespoons of the olive oil, honey, sriracha, and miso, along with a few grinds of black pepper. Add the beef and stir to coat, then cover the bowl and place in the fridge to marinate for 2 to 4 hours.

Preheat the oven to 350°F with a rack in the lower third of the oven.

Put the flour in a bowl. Remove the beef from the marinade (reserve the marinade), pat the beef dry with a paper towel, then season generously with salt and pepper. Toss the beef in the flour to coat, shaking off any excess.

In a Dutch oven, heat the remaining 2 tablespoons olive oil over medium heat. Working in batches, sear the beef on each side until a deep brown crust forms, about 3 minutes per side, adding more oil as needed. Transfer to a plate.

Add the onion, carrots, and garlic to the pot and cook for 3 to 4 minutes, until softened and golden brown in spots. Return the beef and any accumulated juices to the pot, then add the reserved marinade, beef stock, 2½ to 3 cups water (there should be enough liquid to just cover the meat), and bay leaves. Bring to a boil, then reduce to a simmer. Cover and transfer to the oven to braise for 3 hours, or until the meat is very tender. Add a splash of water if needed to keep things saucy. Remove the pot from the oven and fish out the bay leaves. Stir in the peas and parsley and serve.

Try With Wintry Panzanella with Roasted Carrot Ginger Dressing (page 55) or Charred Cabbage with Hoisin Tahini Caesar (page 63).

Spicy Beef
CHOPPED CHEESE

SERVES 4

Whaddaya doin'? I'm walkin' here! Chopped cheese is a quintessential NYC invention and, just like the city, it's messy and sloppy but oh-so wonderful. In my version, spicy Thai flavors fold into the traditional meat mixture for a zingy cheese-studded bite that's all wrapped up in a chewy hoagie roll. Perfect for a laid-back weekend lunch or casual dinner.

TANGY HOISIN MAYO

½ cup Kewpie mayonnaise

1 tablespoon fish sauce

2 teaspoons hoisin sauce

2 teaspoons chili crisp

2 teaspoons fresh lime juice

1 teaspoon toasted sesame oil

Kosher salt

Freshly ground black pepper

EVERYTHING ELSE

1 tablespoon neutral oil

1½ cups diced red onion

6 garlic cloves, minced

1½ pounds ground beef

1½ tablespoons soy sauce

1½ tablespoons fish sauce

1½ tablespoons sriracha

1½ teaspoons ground ginger

1 red chili, thinly sliced, plus more for serving (optional)

Butter, for toasting rolls

4 hoagie or hero rolls, split

12 slices American cheese

1½ cups shredded iceberg lettuce

8 beefsteak tomato slices

Cilantro and mint leaves, for serving

In a small bowl, whisk together the mayonnaise, fish sauce, hoisin sauce, chili crisp, lime juice, and sesame oil. Season with salt and pepper. Cover and place in the fridge. (The hoisin mayo can be made up to 2 days in advance.)

In a large skillet, heat the neutral oil over medium heat until shimmering. Add the onion and cook for 3 to 4 minutes, or until softened and starting to brown on the edges. Add the garlic, beef, soy sauce, fish sauce, sriracha, ginger, and chili (if using). Cook for 3 to 4 minutes, or until the beef is partially cooked, with some pink remaining, and any liquid has mostly been absorbed (it will continue to cook in the next step). Transfer the beef to a bowl.

Wipe the pan clean. Add 1 tablespoon butter and melt over medium heat. Working in batches, toast the cut sides of the rolls until golden brown and warmed through, 1 to 2 minutes, then set aside. Add more butter as needed to toast all the rolls.

Return the beef to the pan, then add the American cheese atop and use two spatulas to "chop" so the cheese is incorporated and melted, gently pressing down on the meat, about 30 seconds.

To assemble each sandwich, spread some hoisin mayo on both sides of a toasted roll, then add lettuce, tomato, sliced chili (if you like), beef mixture, cilantro, and mint. Close the sandwich with the top roll. Wrap each sandwich tightly with wax paper or parchment paper, cut in half, and serve immediately.

Remix! If you can't find hoagie rolls, use sub rolls or soft French bread.

Char Siu
BACON CHEESEBURGER

SERVES 4

When I want a burger, I go all in. My friend Angie Mar's burger at her restaurant, Le B, is the epitome of going all in—but when I can't have hers, I make this one. Here, usual suspects bacon and cheese are present (they are technically optional, so you do you), but now my beloved char siu sauce has been added to the mix. Char siu is a Cantonese-style BBQ sauce—most often found slathered and glistening on big hanging slabs of roasted pork. This particular sauce was perfected with my late dear friend Pam, a native New Yorker whose parents owned a Chinese restaurant in Brooklyn (where a young Barbra Streisand worked!), so she knew of what she spoke. Over the course of a month during the pandemic, we mixed, tasted, and tweaked the recipe together to achieve the right blend. Here, that sauce is used both in the patty and as a spread for the buns. It's so good I've called it gum ho la sauce, which in Cantonese roughly translates to "wow, so good." And that's what this sauce is: part BBQ vibes, part special sauce from you know where.

8 slices thick-cut bacon

CHAR SIU SAUCE

⅓ cup hoisin sauce

¼ cup soy sauce

3 tablespoons Shaoxing wine

2 teaspoons honey

1 teaspoon garlic powder

1 teaspoon ground ginger

1 teaspoon five-spice powder

¼ teaspoon ground white pepper

1½ teaspoons cornstarch

⅛ teaspoon red food coloring (optional)

GUM HO LA SAUCE

⅓ cup Kewpie mayonnaise

2 tablespoons sweet pickle relish

1 teaspoon Dijon mustard

Kosher salt

Freshly ground black pepper

EVERYTHING ELSE

1 pound ground chuck (80% lean)

Kosher salt

Freshly ground black pepper

2 tablespoons neutral oil, plus more as needed

4 slices cheddar cheese

4 sesame buns, split

½ small head iceberg lettuce, shredded

4 tomato slices

1 scallion, green part only, thinly sliced

Preheat the oven to 425°F. Line a rimmed baking sheet with parchment paper or aluminum foil.

Place the bacon on the prepared baking sheet and bake for 15 minutes, or until crisp. Transfer to a paper towel–lined plate to drain.

(recipe continues)

Meanwhile, make the char siu sauce. Combine the hoisin, soy sauce, Shaoxing wine, honey, garlic powder, ginger, five-spice, and white pepper in a small pot. In a small bowl, whisk the cornstarch with 2 tablespoons water until dissolved, and add that to the pot. Bring to a boil over medium heat, then turn the heat down to low and simmer for about 4 minutes, whisking until the sauce has reduced and thickened. Let cool, then stir in the food coloring (if using). (The char siu sauce can be made up to 2 weeks in advance and stored in an airtight container in the refrigerator.)

To make the gum ho la sauce, transfer 2 tablespoons of the char siu sauce to a small bowl and stir in the mayonnaise, pickle relish, and Dijon. Season with ½ teaspoon salt and ¼ teaspoon black pepper and set aside.

In a medium bowl, combine the ground beef, ¼ cup of the char siu sauce, 1 teaspoon salt, and 1 teaspoon black pepper, then use your clean hands to mix until just combined and form into 4 equal patties.

In a large cast-iron skillet or other heavy pan, heat 1 tablespoon of the oil over medium-high heat until shimmering. Add 2 patties to the skillet and press down with the back of a metal spatula a bit to flatten. Cook for 2 minutes, or until browned on the bottom, then flip. Add a slice of cheese atop each patty and cook on the second side for 2 to 2½ minutes. Transfer the patties to a plate. Repeat with the remaining 1 tablespoon oil to cook the remaining 2 patties and 2 slices of cheese.

Add the buns to the skillet, cut sides down, and toast until lightly golden brown, about 1 minute, adding more oil if needed.

To assemble each sandwich, slather the bottom bun with gum ho la sauce, top with lettuce, then a patty, then 2 slices of bacon, then a tomato slice, and finally scallions. Slather more sauce on the top bun and close the sandwich. Serve immediately.

Hot Tip You'll have leftover char siu sauce, which you can slather onto roast chicken or pork, drizzle atop roasted vegetables, add to a stir-fry, mix with noodles—the possibilities are endless.

Try With Summery Corn with Cilantro Lime Vinaigrette (page 41).

Braised Soy and Black Garlic
SHORT RIBS

SERVES 6

This recipe is a low-lift effort (almost zero chopping) with maximum reward. Black garlic is the key ingredient (you can find it at specialty markets or online), and it's truly a game changer. Black garlic is made by aging it until it's a deep black color and the flavor loses most of the acrid funk of fresh garlic—what's left is a sweet, caramelized, umami-packed flavor that's simply mouthwatering. Even better, it can be stored in the fridge for quite a long time. I love serving these ribs with steamed jasmine rice to soak up all that sauce, though who am I kidding—polenta or big slices of sourdough bread would be just as delicious.

5 pounds bone-in short ribs

Kosher salt

Freshly ground black pepper

12 black garlic cloves

¼ cup plus 1 tablespoon dark brown sugar, divided

Neutral oil, for searing

½ cup soy sauce

½ cup rice wine vinegar

1 tablespoon sriracha

4 cups low-sodium beef stock

4 scallions, thinly sliced, for garnish

Grated zest of 1 lemon, for finishing

Flaky sea salt, for finishing

Try With Parm Broccoli with Honey Chili Crisp (page 59).

Remove the short ribs from the refrigerator 30 minutes before cooking. Season on all sides with kosher salt and pepper.

Preheat the oven to 350°F.

Mash the black garlic and 1 tablespoon of the brown sugar in a mortar and pestle until it forms a paste. (Alternatively, you can mash the garlic and brown sugar in a bowl with the back of a spoon.)

In a Dutch oven, heat 1 tablespoon oil over medium-high heat. Working in batches so you don't crowd the pan, add the short ribs and sear on all sides until browned and caramelized, 75 to 90 seconds per side, then transfer to a plate. Add more oil as needed to sear all the ribs. When finished, carefully pour off most of the oil from the Dutch oven.

Return all the short ribs to the Dutch oven and add the black garlic paste, soy sauce, rice wine vinegar, remaining ¼ cup brown sugar, sriracha, and beef stock. If the stock does not cover most of the ribs, add water. Bring to a boil, then cover and place in the oven to roast for 2½ to 3 hours, or until the short ribs are tender and falling off the bone. Uncover and use tongs to move the ribs around a bit. Turn the oven temperature up to 400°F and continue roasting, uncovered, for another 15 to 20 minutes, until the liquid has reduced a bit, the meat is super tender, and everything is a deep, burnished, lovely dark golden brown.

To serve, garnish with the scallions, finish with lemon zest and flaky sea salt, and serve from the Dutch oven.

Hoisin
JUMBO MEATBALLS
with Gochujang Glaze

SERVES 6 TO 8

I'm an impatient person, so I'd rather roll 8 large meatballs than a bunch of small ones—and hey, it's fun! These giants are enrobed in an irresistibly sweet, spicy, and tangy glaze.

3 cups white bread, torn and then cut into very small bite-size pieces

1 cup whole milk

1 pound ground beef chuck (80% lean)

1 pound spicy Italian sausage meat, removed from casings

2 tablespoons hoisin sauce

1 large egg, beaten

½ cup white onion, finely diced

2 tablespoons grated fresh ginger

3 garlic cloves, minced

2 tablespoons minced flat-leaf parsley, plus more for garnish

2 tablespoons minced cilantro, plus more for garnish

1 teaspoon five-spice powder

Kosher salt

Freshly ground black pepper

Steamed jasmine rice or country bread, for serving

GOCHUJANG GLAZE

¼ cup gochujang

3 tablespoons hoisin

2 tablespoons mirin

2 tablespoons honey

1½ teaspoons toasted sesame oil

1 tablespoon rice wine vinegar

1 tablespoon fish sauce

Kosher salt

Freshly ground black pepper

Preheat the oven to 450°F with a rack in the center position.

In a large bowl, combine the bread pieces and milk and stir to coat. Let sit for 5 to 10 minutes.

While the bread is soaking, make the glaze. Combine the gochujang, hoisin, mirin, honey, sesame oil, rice wine vinegar, fish sauce, ½ teaspoon salt, and ¼ teaspoon pepper in a small saucepan and simmer over medium-low heat, stirring frequently, until it reaches a ketchup-like consistency, about 5 minutes.

Once the bread has absorbed all the milk, use a fork (or your impeccably clean hands) to mix it into a somewhat lumpy paste. Add the beef, sausage meat, hoisin, egg, onion, ginger, garlic, parsley, cilantro, five-spice, 1 teaspoon salt, and ½ teaspoon pepper. Use your hands to gently combine the mixture. *(recipe continues)*

Divide the mixture into 8 equal portions (about 1 cup each), then form each portion into a large meatball. Arrange the meatballs in a 9 × 13-inch baking dish, then pour the glaze atop the meatballs, ensuring they are fully coated. Bake for 15 to 20 minutes, or until the glaze is bubbling and the internal temperature is 160°F.

Transfer the balls to a serving platter and pour the glaze from the baking dish atop the meatballs, using a spoon or brush to further coat. Garnish with additional parsley and cilantro and serve with rice or bread alongside.

PORK MEATLOAF
with Salted Egg Yolk

SERVES 4

This is a homestyle Cantonese dish called yook baeng that I grew up eating almost weekly—both Mom and Grandma had it on rotation. Essentially, it's a meatloaf patty using only pork that's steamed and, well, it's delicious. It's rare to find it on a restaurant menu—more often than not you'll see it as the staff family meal, which in my opinion is a very good sign that something's tasty, filling, and pretty easy to make. And I truthfully forgot about this dish for many years until one weekend I was with my family at Harborview restaurant in San Francisco and, as we left, I saw the staff eating it for family meal and all the memories came back to me. Tender pork, hit with a touch of ginger and the crunch of water chestnuts, served atop a bowl of steaming-hot rice— complete and utter meaty comforting perfection. The key here is to aggressively mix the ground pork so that it emulsifies, which creates a super tender patty.

SALTED EGG YOLKS

Table salt, for curing

6 large egg yolks

PORK LOAF

1 pound ground pork sausage meat

1 teaspoon grated fresh ginger

1 tablespoon Shaoxing wine

1½ teaspoons toasted sesame oil

2 teaspoons cornstarch

Kosher salt

¼ teaspoon ground white pepper

⅛ teaspoon baking soda

⅓ cup roughly chopped water chestnuts

⅓ cup finely diced shiitake mushrooms

3 scallions, thinly sliced, white and green parts separated

1 lap cheong link, diced

Steamed jasmine rice, for serving

Pour about ½ inch of table salt into a medium casserole dish or other flat-bottomed container. Use the back of a spoon to create an indent where each yolk will go. Carefully sit the yolks in the indents. Cover with more salt and place in the fridge for 8 hours.

Preheat the oven to 200°F.

Gently rinse the yolks under cold water and use a paper towel to dry— they will be firm but with some give—and place them on a wire rack set over a rimmed baking sheet. Place the sheet in the oven for 1½ hours, or until the yolks are dried and firm. Remove and let cool.

(recipe continues)

In the bowl of a stand mixer fitted with the paddle attachment (or in a large bowl with chopsticks), combine the pork, ginger, 3 tablespoons water, Shaoxing wine, sesame oil, cornstarch, 1 teaspoon kosher salt, white pepper, and baking soda and mix for 5 to 7 minutes on medium speed until the mixture is very smooth and emulsified and the meat starts to get white and creamy. Fold in the water chestnuts, shiitake mushrooms, and scallion whites. Transfer to a shallow pie pan (or heatproof shallow bowl) and pat gently into an even layer. Top with the lap cheong.

Place a steamer rack in a wide pot (the pot should be slightly wider than the pie pan so that the steam can escape) and fill with 1 inch water. Set the pie pan on the rack and cover. When the water comes to a boil, steam for 15 minutes. Turn off the heat and let sit, covered, for 10 minutes.

Carefully remove the pie pan from the steamer, grate 2 or 3 salted egg yolks atop, garnish with the scallion greens, and serve with steamed jasmine rice.

Mix In Top with Quick Pickled Cukes (page 22).

Hot Tip The leftover salted egg yolks can be stored in an airtight container in the fridge for up to 3 months.

Remix! No time for salted egg yolks? Add slices of 7-minute eggs or century eggs atop before serving.

Sweet and Sour
STICKY RIBS
with Citrus Peanut Gremolata

SERVES 6 TO 8

This is my ode to a favorite: Chinese pork ribs (paai gwat). They're usually lightly burnished with a sticky, sweet-savory coating, but I've decided to shake things up and give 'em the sweet and sour treatment. A rich, tangy sauce enrobes juicy fall-off-the-bone tender meat, and then everything is crowned with a refreshing herbaceous gremolata, punctuated by the crunch of peanuts.

RIBS

1 tablespoon five-spice powder

2 teaspoons smoked paprika

2 teaspoons onion powder

1 teaspoon garlic powder

Kosher salt

Freshly ground black pepper

½ teaspoon cayenne powder

1 (4-pound) rack baby back pork ribs

1 tablespoon extra-virgin olive oil

¾ cup beer, apple cider, or water

SWEET AND SOUR SAUCE

¼ cup ketchup

¼ cup rice wine vinegar

3 tablespoons soy sauce

1 tablespoon maple syrup

1 tablespoon sriracha

Kosher salt

2 to 3 drops red food coloring (optional)

2 teaspoons cornstarch

GREMOLATA

Grated zest of 1 orange

Grated zest of 1 lemon

Grated zest of 1 lime

½ cup minced flat-leaf parsley

¼ cup chopped roasted salted peanuts

1 tablespoon extra-virgin olive oil

Preheat the oven to 275°F. Line a rimmed baking sheet or roasting pan with aluminum foil.

In a small bowl, combine the five-spice, paprika, onion powder, garlic powder, 2 teaspoons salt, 1 teaspoon black pepper, and cayenne and mix to combine. Rub the rack of ribs with the olive oil, then coat completely with the spice rub on all sides, patting with your hands to make it adhere.

Place the rack bone side down on the prepared baking sheet (if your rack is large, cut it in half). Add the beer to the pan, taking care not to pour it onto the rack. Cover tightly with aluminum foil and roast for 2 hours.

Meanwhile, make the sweet and sour sauce. In a small saucepan, combine the ketchup, rice wine vinegar, soy sauce, maple syrup, sriracha, ½ teaspoon salt, and food coloring (if using). In a small bowl, mix the cornstarch with 1 tablespoon water until completely combined, then pour the mixture into the saucepan. Bring to a simmer over medium-low heat and simmer for 1 to 2 minutes, until thickened. Remove from the heat and set aside.

Remove the foil, turn the ribs bone side up, and brush generously with the sweet and sour sauce. Turn the oven temperature up to 400°F and roast, uncovered, for 20 minutes, flipping the ribs and slathering with more sauce every 5 minutes.

Turn the broiler on high. Brush more sauce on the meaty side of the ribs and broil for 2 to 3 minutes, or until the sauce is bubbling and starting to darken. Remove the ribs from the oven and brush one final coat of glaze on top. Let rest for 15 minutes.

While the ribs are resting, make the gremolata. In a small bowl, combine the orange zest, lemon zest, lime zest, parsley, peanuts, and olive oil.

Cut the rack into individual ribs. Sprinkle with the gremolata and serve with more sweet and sour sauce alongside.

Try With Crispy Deviled Tea Eggs (page 6) or Honeydew and Cucumber with Halloumi and Togarashi Hot Honey (page 42) for a summery meal.

Hot Tip The gremolata is also great with fish or roasted vegetables.

Crispy
PORK BELLY SLIDERS
with Pineapple Lime Aioli

MAKES
10 SLIDERS

The pork in this recipe is the classic Cantonese siu yuk (which literally means "roast meat"). Its signature is the almost shatteringly crispy skin atop fatty, tender, supple meat. The process does take some time (you start it the day before), but you will be rewarded in spades. While you can of course eat the pork belly unadorned (and you will, trust me—it's so good!), I like to slide the meat into Hawaiian buns slathered with a simple but brightly acidic aioli, which is the perfect balance to the rich meat.

SIU YUK

1½ pounds skin-on pork belly strips

2 teaspoons Shaoxing wine

½ teaspoon neutral oil

½ teaspoon five-spice powder

½ teaspoon garlic powder

½ teaspoon ground white pepper

Kosher salt

1 teaspoon rice wine vinegar

¼ cup coarse salt

PINEAPPLE LIME AIOLI

½ cup Kewpie mayonnaise

¼ cup canned crushed pineapple, drained, plus 2 teaspoons juice from the can

1 teaspoon grated lime zest

Kosher salt

Freshly ground black pepper

EVERYTHING ELSE

10 Hawaiian rolls, split

Bread and butter pickles, for serving

Cilantro, for garnish

Pat the pork belly dry with a paper towel, then place it skin side down on a cutting board. Rub the meat with the Shaoxing wine, oil, five-spice, garlic powder, white pepper, and ¼ teaspoon kosher salt. Turn the pork over and use a very sharp knife to score the skin in a grid pattern at ¼-inch intervals, ensuring you cut through only the top skin layer, not the fat or flesh. Place the pork belly in a container, skin side up, and dab the skin with a paper towel. Leave in the fridge, uncovered, for 12 to 24 hours.

Preheat the oven to 375°F with a rack in the lower third of the oven. Line a baking dish with aluminum foil; it should be small enough to fit the meat snugly in a single layer so that they are all touching.

Place the pork skin side up in the prepared baking dish. If you need to, use the foil to create "walls" around the pork belly so that the flesh is covered and only the top skin is exposed. Brush the skin with the rice wine vinegar, then pack the prepared skin side with the coarse salt. Place in the oven and roast for 1 hour.

Remove the salt layer (it should easily come off in large chunks), and turn the broiler on high. Broil for 10 to 14 minutes, or until the skin is deep golden brown, blistered, and crispy. Let rest for 10 to 15 minutes.

While the pork is resting, make the aioli. Combine the mayonnaise, crushed pineapple and juice, and lime zest in a medium bowl. Season with salt and pepper.

Cut the pork into ¼- to ⅓-inch-thick slices. To assemble the sliders, slather aioli on the bottom rolls, add 1 slice of pork to each, drizzle with a bit of pork jus, top with a bread and butter pickle and some cilantro, and serve.

Remix! Most Chinese delis and food counters sell siu yuk, so if you're short on time, go ahead and buy some ready-made. Be sure to ask for cuts that don't have a lot of fat on them.

CHICKPEA BOURGUIGNON

SERVES 4 TO 6

When you're in the mood for rich flavors without the heavy baggage, this dish does the job in spades. This vegetarian riff on the rustic French classic beef bourguignon has all its hallmarks, but now we're rolling with tender chickpeas and ditching the beef. It's hearty and rustic and something I'll make on Sunday and eat all week, and just like the original, the flavors develop and deepen as they mingle, so double-win in my book.

1 tablespoon extra-virgin olive oil

2 medium carrots, sliced ¼ inch thick

1 large white onion, diced into ½-inch pieces

5 garlic cloves, minced

½ teaspoon smoked paprika

Kosher salt

Freshly ground black pepper

2 tablespoons tomato paste

1 tablespoon white or yellow miso

4 or 5 thyme sprigs

2 (15-ounce) cans chickpeas, drained and rinsed

7 ounces frozen pearl onions

1 tablespoon all-purpose flour

1 cup dry red wine

1 cup low-sodium vegetable broth

2 bay leaves

2 tablespoons unsalted butter

8 ounces button or baby bella mushrooms, sliced

¼ cup roughly chopped flat-leaf parsley

In a Dutch oven or large skillet with high sides, heat the olive oil over medium heat. Add the carrots, onion, garlic, and smoked paprika, season with salt and pepper, and sauté until the onion is soft and the carrots are just tender, 4 to 5 minutes. Add the tomato paste, miso, and thyme, stir to combine, and cook for 2 to 3 minutes. Add the chickpeas, pearl onions, and flour and stir. Season with salt and pepper. Add the wine, broth, and bay leaves. Cover and simmer, stirring occasionally, for 10 minutes, then uncover and cook for another 10 minutes, or until the sauce is reduced and the chickpeas are tender.

In the meantime, melt the butter in another skillet over medium-high heat. Add the mushrooms and sauté for 7 to 8 minutes, or until they're crispy and browned.

Remove and discard the bay leaves from the Dutch oven. Add the mushrooms and parsley, stir to combine, and serve.

MAPO EGGPLANT

SERVES 4

This vegetarian take on Sichuan mapo tofu swaps out the traditional ground beef for meaty eggplant. It's easy to multiply for company and even better the next day as the flavors have melded and developed even more. Where's the beef? Who cares!

1 (14- to 16-ounce) block firm or extra-firm tofu

1 large globe eggplant, trimmed and cut into ½-inch cubes

3 tablespoons neutral oil, divided

Kosher salt

Freshly ground black pepper

3 garlic cloves, grated or finely minced

1 tablespoon grated or finely minced fresh ginger

3 scallions, sliced, white and green parts separated

¼ cup chili crisp

2 tablespoons fermented chili bean paste

2 teaspoons light soy sauce

½ teaspoon ground Sichuan peppercorns or white peppercorns

1 tablespoon cornstarch

1 teaspoon sugar

Steamed jasmine rice, for serving

Preheat the oven to 425°F. Line a rimmed baking sheet with parchment paper.

Place the tofu block on a plate lined with 4 layers of paper towel. Add 4 more layers of paper towel on the tofu, then place a small cutting board on top. Place a large can of tomatoes or soup atop the board and let sit for 10 to 15 minutes, or until most of the liquid has been pressed out of the tofu. Cut the tofu into ½-inch cubes and set aside.

Put the eggplant on the prepared baking sheet, drizzle with 2 table-spoons of the oil, season with salt and pepper, and toss to coat. Roast for 25 to 30 minutes, tossing halfway through and rotating the pan, or until the eggplant is brown, crisped, and cooked through.

In a Dutch oven or large skillet with high sides, heat the remaining 1 ta-blespoon oil over medium heat until shimmering. Add the garlic, gin-ger, scallion whites, chili crisp, fermented chili bean paste, soy sauce, and Sichuan peppercorns and mix to combine. Cook for 2 to 3 minutes, stirring frequently, until the mixture is sizzling, fragrant, and toasty. In a small bowl, mix the cornstarch with 2 tablespoons water until completely combined, then pour the mixture into the Dutch oven, along with the sugar and 1 cup water, and cook for 1 minute, stirring frequently, until combined.

Add the roasted eggplant and mix to combine. Add the tofu and gently mix to combine. Turn the heat down to medium-low and simmer for 4 to 5 minutes, or until heated through and the flavors are melded. Stir in the scallion greens, reserving some for garnish. Transfer to a serving platter, garnish with the reserved scallion greens, and serve with steamed jas-mine rice.

Hot Tip The key to preparing firm or extra-firm tofu is to get some of the liquid out of it. Tofu comes stored in water (and is made up of about 80 percent water itself), so taking the time to press out some of that water will yield a more tender bite. Don't press for any longer than 10 or 15 minutes, though, or too much water will be extracted, resulting in a tougher, drier texture.

FAMILY STYLE

The Big Easy

MUSHROOM STRATA

SERVES 8 TO 10

Taking the time to make this strata is worth every moment. The result is a generous, golden-brown beauty that will feed a crowd. In fact, it was one of the first things I learned how to make in NYC (along with my Big Beautiful Beef Stew, page 166) because it fed a crowd, was essentially a one-dish meal, and was universally welcomed for brunch or dinner. And incidentally, any leftovers heat up beautifully. This recipe can easily be halved to serve fewer people; use an 8-inch square baking pan or a 2-quart casserole dish.

2 tablespoons unsalted butter, plus more for the pan

1 (1-pound) boule sourdough bread, cut into 1-inch cubes (about 8 cups)

1 large shallot, diced

2 garlic cloves, minced

1 pound mushrooms, sliced

2 tablespoons thyme leaves, minced

Kosher salt

Freshly ground black pepper

3 ounces baby spinach

1 cup frozen peas

2 teaspoons oyster sauce

1¾ cups grated Gruyère (about 5 ounces), divided

1½ cups grated mozzarella (about 6 ounces)

8 large eggs

2 cups whole milk

8 ounces cream cheese, at room temperature

2 tablespoons white or yellow miso

1 tablespoon Dijon mustard

½ teaspoon ground nutmeg

½ teaspoon ground allspice

Preheat the oven to 400°F with a rack in the center position. Butter a 9 × 13-inch baking dish and set aside.

Spread out the sourdough in a single layer on a rimmed baking sheet and bake until golden brown, tossing halfway through, about 10 minutes. Remove from the oven and set aside. Turn the oven down to 350°F.

In a large sauté pan or cast-iron skillet, melt the butter over medium-high heat. Add the shallot, garlic, mushrooms, and thyme, season with salt and pepper, and sauté until the mushrooms are tender, about 4 minutes. Stir in the spinach and cook until wilted, about 2 minutes, then stir in the peas and oyster sauce and cook until the peas are warmed through, about 2 minutes. Transfer everything to the buttered baking dish and let cool for 5 minutes. Add the toasted bread, 1½ cups of the Gruyère, and the mozzarella to the sauté pan and toss to combine.

In a large blender (48-ounce capacity or larger), combine the eggs, milk, cream cheese, miso, Dijon, nutmeg, and allspice, season with salt and pepper, and blend until smooth. (Alternatively, combine the ingredients in a large bowl and use a hand mixer or whisk.)

To assemble, transfer the bread mixture to the prepared baking dish, then pour the egg mixture atop. Press the bread down to submerge it as much as possible in the egg mixture.

Cover with aluminum foil and bake for 45 minutes, or until the edges are set but the center is still slightly wobbly, then uncover and bake for another 25 minutes, or until the top is deep golden brown and the middle is just set. Sprinkle with the remaining ¼ cup Gruyère and bake for another 5 minutes, or until the cheese is melted and bubbly. Remove from the oven and let stand for 10 minutes, then slice and serve.

Sweet and Sour
SPICY TOFU *and* CHICKPEAS

SERVES 4

I would be remiss to not include a few sweet and sour recipes in this book (also check out my Sweet and Sour Sticky Ribs on page 182), as this mouthwatering combination was always my most requested dish at any family banquet growing up. While my mom conferred in hushed confident tones with the waiter about which fish was freshest and which vegetable was crispest and if the winter melon soup was good that night, I'd pipe up and murmur, "Can we get the sweet and sour pork?" It was a dish that we never made at home—much too much sugar and also very standard run-of-the-mill fare in Mom's opinion. But she would relent and order it with a sigh. And yes, I still love it to this day. But here is a lighter, meat-free take. I've draped that signature silky sauce on crispy tofu and added the tender bite of chickpeas, along with a shower of herbs and a squeeze of lime for freshness.

TOFU AND CHICKPEAS

1 (14- to 16-ounce) block extra-firm tofu

2 scallions, green parts only

1 tablespoon soy sauce

⅓ cup cornstarch

1 tablespoon five-spice powder

Kosher salt

Freshly ground black pepper

¼ cup plus 1 tablespoon neutral oil

1 (15-ounce) can chickpeas, drained and rinsed

½ cup mix of mint leaves, cilantro, and flat-leaf parsley leaves

Lime wedges, for serving

Steamed jasmine rice, for serving

SWEET AND SOUR SAUCE

¼ cup ketchup

¼ cup rice wine vinegar

3 tablespoons soy sauce

1 tablespoon maple syrup

1 tablespoon sriracha

2 teaspoons cornstarch

Kosher salt

2 to 3 drops red food coloring (optional)

Place the tofu block on a plate lined with 4 layers of paper towel. Add 4 more layers of paper towel on the tofu, then place a small cutting board on top. Place a large can of tomatoes or soup atop the board and let sit for 10 to 15 minutes, or until most of the liquid has been pressed out of the tofu.

In the meantime, make the sweet and sour sauce. In a small bowl, mix the ketchup, rice wine vinegar, soy sauce, maple syrup, sriracha, 3 table-

(recipe continues)

spoons water, cornstarch, ½ teaspoon salt, and food coloring (if using) until smooth and combined. Set aside.

Julienne the scallion greens and plunge into a bowl of ice water until they curl. Remove and place on a paper towel to drain.

Cut the tofu into 1-inch cubes. In a large bowl, toss the tofu with the soy sauce. Add the cornstarch and five-spice powder, season with salt and pepper, and gently toss, ensuring the tofu is coated on all sides with the cornstarch.

Heat ¼ cup of the oil in a cast-iron or nonstick skillet over medium-high heat until shimmering. Add the tofu cubes in a single layer, working in batches if necessary to ensure they don't touch. Cook until golden brown, 3 to 4 minutes, then use chopsticks or tongs to turn them over and cook on a second side for 4 minutes. Transfer the tofu to a plate.

Wipe the pan clean and return to the stove over medium-low heat. Add the chickpeas and sweet and sour sauce. Once the chickpeas are warmed and the sauce is bubbling, about 1 minute, return the tofu to the pan and mix quickly, until the tofu and chickpeas are just coated with the sauce, then immediately transfer to a serving platter.

Garnish with the prepared scallion, herbs, and lime wedges, and serve immediately with rice.

Try With Super Fresh Snap Pea Salad (page 45).

CRISPY TOFU
with Charred Scallion Pesto

SERVES 4

Tofu is a go-to—it's full of protein and can take on any flavor like a culinary chameleon. While there are many kinds of tofu, more often than not I lean toward firm or extra-firm tofu because of its versatility and ease of use. Sliced or cubed, steamed or fried, it does it all. In this case we go for texture, with a thin coating of cornstarch and pan-fried till crispy on the outside and firm but giving on the inside, and paired with the verdant peppery zip of a super easy scallion pesto.

1 (14- to 16-ounce) block firm or extra-firm tofu

⅓ cup cornstarch

½ teaspoon ground ginger

½ teaspoon ground coriander

¼ teaspoon smoked paprika

Kosher salt

Freshly ground black pepper

2 tablespoons neutral oil

Grated zest of 1 lemon

Flaky sea salt, for finishing

1 scallion, thinly sliced

PESTO

1 bunch scallions, trimmed

1 cup packed flat-leaf parsley

⅓ cup freshly grated Pecorino Romano cheese

⅓ cup roasted cashews

3 tablespoons fresh lemon juice

½ cup extra-virgin olive oil

Kosher salt

Freshly ground black pepper

Preheat the broiler on high with a rack in the upper third of the oven.

Place the tofu on a plate lined with 4 layers of paper towel. Add 4 more layers of paper towel on the tofu, then place a small cutting board on top. Place a large can of tomatoes or soup atop the board and let sit for 10 to 15 minutes, or until most of the liquid has been pressed out of the tofu. Cut the tofu into ¾-inch slabs, then cut each slab on the diagonal into a triangle.

Meanwhile, make the pesto. Spread out the scallions in a single layer on a rimmed baking sheet and broil for 3 to 4 minutes, then flip and broil for another 3 to 4 minutes, or until tender and charred dark brown in spots. Remove from the oven and turn the oven to 400°F.

Transfer the scallions to a food processor, along with the parsley, Pecorino Romano, cashews, and lemon juice. Pulse a few times to break things up, then turn on the processor and stream in the olive oil until just combined to a smooth consistency but still with a bit of texture. Season with 1 teaspoon kosher salt and ½ teaspoon pepper and transfer to a bowl. (The pesto can be made up to 5 days in advance and stored in an airtight container in the fridge.)

Line a rimmed baking sheet with parchment paper.

In a medium bowl, mix the cornstarch, ginger, coriander, paprika, kosher salt, and pepper. Coat each tofu slice in neutral oil, then toss in the cornstarch mixture, ensuring all sides are coated and pressing lightly to help it adhere. Arrange the tofu on the prepared baking sheet and bake for 30 minutes, flipping the tofu halfway through, or until golden brown and crisp.

(recipe continues)

To serve, swirl the pesto on a serving platter, then arrange the tofu on top. Finish with lemon zest and flaky sea salt. Garnish with the scallion and serve immediately.

Hot Tip Spoon the charred scallion pesto over scrambled eggs, fish, or meat.

Try With Charred Carrots with Gochujang Honey Butter (page 72) or Golden Fried Rice (page 82).

A happy and dapper Grandma and Grandpa, circa late-1940s, Hong Kong.

Chilled
SUMMER TOFU

SERVES 4

My mom served this dish often for company as it was essentially all pantry ingredients and ready in minutes. Delicate silken tofu is topped with a quick soy dressing and adorned with lots of herbs and pickled ginger. The special ingredient? Century eggs (also known as thousand-year-old eggs—I know 100 and 1,000 are not the same. A misnomer all for dramatic effect!), which are available in Asian grocery stores or online. These preserved eggs have a deep, rich flavor, a touch earthy and full of umami. While Mom served this dish year-round, I prefer it in the hot summer months, when turning on the stove is out of the question.

1 scallion

1 (14- to 16-ounce) block silken tofu

3 tablespoons soy sauce

1 tablespoon toasted sesame oil

1 teaspoon chili oil, or more, if you like

½ teaspoon sugar

½ teaspoon five-spice powder

Kosher salt

⅛ teaspoon ground white pepper

2 tablespoons pickled ginger

1 red chili, thinly sliced (optional)

1 mini cucumber, cut into ¼-inch slices

2 century eggs, peeled and cut into quarters

Cilantro leaves and tender stems, for garnish

Trim and cut the scallion into thirds, then julienne into thin strips. Plunge the strips into a bowl of ice water for 2 to 3 minutes, or until they curl, then place on a paper towel to drain.

Gently pat the tofu dry with a paper towel and place on a small platter with a lip. Score the tofu in a ½- to ¾-inch grid, cutting only approximately ¼ inch down.

In a small bowl, mix the soy sauce, sesame oil, chili oil, sugar, five-spice, ¼ teaspoon salt, and white pepper.

Arrange the pickled ginger atop the tofu, along with half the prepared scallions. Arrange the red chili (if using) and cucumber on the platter around the tofu. Pour the sauce atop all. Arrange the century eggs and remaining scallions alongside the tofu. Garnish with the cilantro and serve chilled.

Hot Tip The curly scallion method is purely decorative—plunging them into ice water makes them curl, all the better to stack up a big pile atop your tofu! If you like, skip this step and thinly slice them on a diagonal.

Another Hot Tip Make the scallions (store in a jar filled with water) and sauce (store in an airtight container) the day before and refrigerate until ready to serve.

Remix! This dish is just as delicious without the century eggs—omit them or add 7-minute eggs instead.

(Not Too Sweet)
Sweets

When biting into a dessert, my grandma's ultimate compliment was "Hmm, very good, not too sweet." And the same phrase holds true for my mom too. Overly sugared American desserts are in direct contrast to Cantonese desserts from Hong Kong, which are more like a brief coda at the end of the meal, a small bite rather than a big finale. Dessert was not a "thing" in our home. Sweets, in fact, were few and far between. My mom, the self-proclaimed health nut, was not a baker and kept sugar and anything processed far away from my sister and me. Candy bars and soft drinks? Nope. Brownies and cookies? Not a chance. When asked what was for dessert, she'd point over to the fruit basket where a few bananas and a Red Delicious apple awaited my forlorn gaze. However, when we did indulge in sweets, it was always the best. That was my mom's philosophy—cheesecakes and tarts from the local bakery in Mill Valley, seasonal strawberry pies, croissants from her preferred spot in San Francisco. And at dim sum on weekends, I would always get my favorites— jin deui (fried sesame balls filled with sweet bean paste) and dan taat (egg custard tartlets).

The desserts in this chapter are not complicated. I've worked to cull the steps down to the essentials, while designing them for maximum flavor and impact ('cause let's face it, we want our desserts to be impressive, am I right?). In some cases I've played with riffs on some of my favorite Chinese sweets, like my Dan Taat Phyllo Tart (page 222), and other times my mom's love of French food comes through, like with my Coffee Basque Cheesecake with Gingersnap Black Tea Crust (page 211). But in all cases it's about deliciously simple desserts that serve as the final bite to a meal. So very good, and not too sweet.

APPLE CAKE
with Salted Maple Caramel

SERVES 15

"Should I make apple cake?" Grandma would ask. The answer was always a resounding chorus of yes. Of all the sweets I remember Grandma making, apple cake is at the top. The memory of arriving at her apartment to the aroma of warm apple cake was a joy that my sister and I shared with anticipatory fervor. Apple-packed, with just enough cake to hold everything together, it was the perfect (and rare) sweet treat for us kids. Simple and delicious. I've gilded the lily (or rather, the apple) with a quick salted maple caramel to drizzle atop.

Unsalted butter, for the pan

1½ cups light brown sugar

½ cup neutral oil

½ cup cold-pressed coconut oil

3 large eggs, at room temperature

1 teaspoon vanilla extract

2 cups all-purpose flour

1 teaspoon baking powder

½ teaspoon baking soda

Kosher salt

1 teaspoon ground cinnamon

½ teaspoon five-spice powder

3 cups ½-inch diced apples

1 cup roughly chopped toasted walnuts

Vanilla ice cream, for serving (optional)

SALTED HONEY CARAMEL

¼ cup unsalted European-style butter

½ cup plus 2 tablespoons maple syrup

1 cup heavy cream

Kosher salt

Preheat the oven to 350°F. Butter a 9 x 13-inch baking dish or a 10-inch round cake dish and line with parchment paper.

In a large bowl, beat the brown sugar, neutral oil, coconut oil, eggs, and vanilla until well combined. Sift the flour, baking powder, baking soda, 1 teaspoon salt, cinnamon, and five-spice directly into the bowl. Mix until just combined. Fold in the apples and walnuts.

Transfer to the prepared baking dish and bake for 40 to 45 minutes, or until a toothpick inserted into the center comes out clean. Remove from the oven and cool in the pan on a wire rack.

Meanwhile, make the caramel. Melt the butter and maple syrup in a small saucepan over medium heat. Bring to a simmer and let simmer for 10 minutes, or until the color has darkened just slightly. Add the cream and whisk to combine. Bring to a boil, then remove the pan from the heat. Stir in 1 teaspoon salt, then transfer to a small bowl or jar, cover, and place in the fridge to cool completely. (The caramel can be made up to 5 days ahead of time.)

To serve, slice the cake into squares and top with ice cream, if you like. Pour the caramel into a small serving bowl and serve alongside to drizzle atop.

Hot Tip Use any firm, tart baking apple, such as Granny Smith, Fuji, Honeygold, Gala, or Braeburn.

Remix! Try it with peaches or other stone fruit, or with cubed mango or pineapple. Frozen fruits work well too. Keep them frozen while working with them—the oven will do all the work.

Summer Berry
SNACK CAKE

SERVES 6

If there was ever a no-brainer cake to make for no reason at all (which is sometimes the best reason), here it is. The spices add a warming back note, while the miso's earthy flavors balance out—and complement—the sweetness of the berries. This is one of those cakes that can be whipped up on the fly and studded with practically any fruit you might have on hand. And you know, a slice in the morning with coffee is just as delightful as a slice after dinner with some whipped cream or ice cream—so have at it!

1 cup (2 sticks) unsalted butter, softened, plus more for the pan

1¾ cups all-purpose flour

1¾ teaspoons baking powder

Kosher salt

¼ teaspoon ground cardamom

¼ teaspoon ground ginger

1¼ cups white sugar

2 tablespoons grated lime zest

2 tablespoons grated lemon zest

2 tablespoons yellow miso

2 large eggs

1 teaspoon vanilla extract

½ cup full-fat Greek yogurt

1 pint raspberries

1 pint blackberries

2 tablespoons turbinado sugar

Preheat the oven to 350°F with a rack in the lower third of the oven. Butter a 9-inch round cake pan and line with parchment paper.

In a medium bowl, whisk together the flour, baking powder, ¾ teaspoon salt, cardamom, and ginger.

Use a handheld mixer (or stand mixer fitted with the paddle attachment) to beat the butter on medium speed until smooth, about 2 minutes. Add the white sugar, lime zest, lemon zest, and miso and continue to beat until pale green and fluffy, about 3 minutes, scraping down the sides of the bowl as needed.

Add the eggs one at a time, then add the vanilla and Greek yogurt. Turn the mixer to low (or switch to a spatula), add the flour mixture, and mix until just combined. At this point the batter will look curdled and broken—don't worry!

Fold in half the raspberries and half the blackberries, then transfer the batter to the prepared cake pan (the batter will be quite thick). Use a knife or offset spatula to level the top. Dot the batter with the remaining raspberries and blackberries. Sprinkle with the turbinado sugar.

Bake for 10 minutes (it will just start to puff up), then turn the oven temperature down to 325°F and bake for another 45 to 50 minutes, or until a toothpick inserted into the center comes out with only a few crumbs attached.

Let cool for 20 minutes in the pan on a wire rack, then carefully turn out of the pan onto the rack and let sit until fully cooled. Slice and serve.

Miso Roasted Carrot
SLAB CAKE *with*
Citrus Cream Cheese Frosting

SERVES 12

Roasting the carrots is an extra step, I'll admit, but trust me—taking the time to sweetly caramelize those carrots will bring out their carroty essence even more, which equals a greater complexity and depth of flavor. Grandma's recipe notebook has a myriad of carrot cake recipes; this is my take on them.

CARROT PUREE

3 medium carrots (8 to 10 ounces), cut into ½-inch pieces

2 tablespoons extra-virgin olive oil

3 tablespoons white miso

2 tablespoons maple syrup

Kosher salt

CAKE

Unsalted butter, for the pan

1½ cups all-purpose flour, plus more for the pan

2 teaspoons baking powder

¼ teaspoon baking soda

½ teaspoon five-spice powder

½ teaspoon ground cinnamon

Kosher salt

1 cup white sugar

⅓ cup dark brown sugar

3 large eggs

2 teaspoons yellow miso

1 orange, zested and supremed (see Hot Tip on page 60)

¾ cup extra-virgin olive oil

1 teaspoon vanilla extract

2 cups shredded carrots (about 2 large carrots)

½ cup golden raisins

1 cup roughly chopped toasted walnuts, plus more for decoration

CITRUS CREAM CHEESE FROSTING

12 ounces cream cheese, at room temperature

6 tablespoons unsalted butter, at room temperature

1 teaspoon vanilla extract

Grated zest of 1 orange

Grated zest of 1 lemon

3 cups confectioners' sugar, sifted

Preheat the oven to 350°F.

To make the carrot puree, put the carrots in a small baking dish. In a small bowl, whisk together the olive oil, miso, maple syrup, and ½ teaspoon salt, then toss the carrots with the mixture until evenly coated. Cover with aluminum foil and roast for 15 minutes, then uncover and roast for another 15 minutes, or until darkened and almost charred in spots. In a blender, puree the carrots until smooth, then transfer to a bowl and let cool. Leave the oven on.

Butter a 9 x 13-inch baking dish, dust with a light coating of flour, tap out the excess, and set aside.

In a medium bowl, whisk together the flour, baking powder, baking soda, five-spice, cinnamon, and ¼ teaspoon salt.

In the bowl of a stand mixer fitted with the whisk attachment, combine the white sugar, brown sugar, eggs, miso, and half the orange zest (reserve the other half for decoration) and whip on high until the mixture is pale, smooth, and thick, 4 to 5 minutes. Turn the speed down to medium, add the olive oil, vanilla, and 1 cup of the carrot puree, and mix until just combined.

Use a spatula to fold in the flour mixture until just combined. Then fold in the shredded carrots, golden raisins, and walnuts. Roughly chop the orange segments and gently fold in. Pour the batter into the prepared baking dish and bake for 40 minutes, or until the cake is browned and a toothpick inserted into the center comes out with only a few crumbs attached.

Place the pan on a wire rack and let cool completely.

To make the frosting, combine the cream cheese, butter, vanilla, orange zest, and lemon zest in the bowl of a stand mixer fitted with the whisk attachment and blend on high until smooth. Add the confectioners' sugar and mix on low at first, then increase the speed to high and whip until smooth.

When the cake is completely cooled, frost the top of the cake and use a knife or offset spatula to push the frosting to the edges of the pan. Decorate with the reserved orange zest and walnuts, slice into squares, and serve.

Coffee
BASQUE CHEESECAKE
with Gingersnap Black Tea Crust

SERVES 8 TO 10

I love using tea leaves in desserts—they add a complex, slightly bitter herbaceous note that's a great counterpoint to the inherent sweetness going on. Here the classic Basque cheesecake, with its characteristic dark brown caramelized top—normally crustless—gets a crust (pulling inspo from New York–style cheesecakes here) for a bit of crunch in the form of gingersnaps studded with black tea leaves. A perfect complement to the espresso-infused custard. Not a bad way to offer up coffee and tea, am I right?

CRUST

Unsalted butter, for the pan

10 ounces gingersnaps

2 tablespoons brown sugar

1 tablespoon white sugar

2 teaspoons black tea leaves
(2 tea bags)

Kosher salt

6 tablespoons unsalted butter,
melted

CUSTARD

2 tablespoons instant espresso
granules, divided

6 tablespoons brewed
espresso, at room temperature

2 pounds cream cheese,
at room temperature

1½ cups white sugar

6 large eggs

2 cups heavy cream

1 teaspoon vanilla extract

Kosher salt

⅓ cup all-purpose flour

Preheat the oven to 400°F. Butter a 9-inch springform pan, then line the sides with a parchment paper collar that reaches at least 2 inches above the pan.

In a food processor, pulse the gingersnaps until you have crumbs, then add the brown sugar, white sugar, tea leaves, and ½ teaspoon salt and pulse a few times to combine. Add the melted butter and pulse 4 or 5 times, until fully combined and the mixture resembles wet sand. Pour the mixture into the prepared pan and use the bottom of a cup to press it into an even, flat layer. Bake for 10 minutes, or until fragrant and the crust starts to take a bit of color. Remove from the oven and let cool. Leave the oven on.

To make the custard, add 1 tablespoon instant espresso granules to the brewed espresso and stir to dissolve; set aside. In the bowl of a stand mixer fitted with the paddle attachment, beat the cream cheese on medium speed until smooth. Add the white sugar and continue to mix, scraping down the sides of the bowl as needed. Add the eggs, one at a time, and beat until fully incorporated. Add the cream, vanilla, espresso mixture, and 1 teaspoon salt and beat until combined and smooth with no lumps. Sift the flour directly into the bowl, then add the remaining 1 tablespoon espresso granules and mix on low, scraping down the sides of the bowl as needed, until just combined and smooth.

(recipe continues)

Pour the batter onto the crust in the pan and tap a few times on the countertop to remove any air bubbles. Place on a rimmed baking sheet and bake for 60 to 65 minutes, or until the top is dark golden brown and almost burnt and the center is slightly jiggly (it will continue to firm up as the cake cools).

Place the pan on a wire rack to cool completely, then refrigerate until firm (at least 4 to 5 hours, but overnight is even better). To serve, remove the sides of the pan and peel off the parchment, then transfer the cake to a serving platter and slice.

Remix! If you can't find gingersnaps, use graham crackers plus ½ teaspoon ground ginger.

CHOCOLATE HOISIN CAKE *with Fluffy Frosting*

SERVES 6 TO 8

Woefully, I was allergic to chocolate as a child—a setback I outgrew most likely out of sheer force of will so I could experience the rich, malted, candied, tender joy of a slice of chocolate cake like this. To bump up that chocolate experience, I've added not only instant espresso powder, but also hoisin sauce—you heard me right—which adds a deep, rich background note of flavor. The frosting brings both tang and lightness, and is stabilized due to the cream cheese and cornstarch so it won't start weeping or deflating as plain whipped cream would.

CAKE

Unsalted butter, for the pan

2 large eggs

1 cup light brown sugar

1 cup sour cream

1 tablespoon hoisin sauce

1 teaspoon vanilla extract

1 teaspoon instant espresso powder

Kosher salt

1 cup all-purpose flour

¾ cup unsweetened cocoa powder

1 teaspoon baking powder

½ teaspoon baking soda

¾ cup brewed hot strong coffee

Dark chocolate shavings, for garnish (optional)

FLUFFY FROSTING

3 cups heavy cream

8 ounces cream cheese, at room temperature

1½ cups confectioners' sugar

2 teaspoons cornstarch

1 teaspoon vanilla extract

Preheat the oven to 350°F. Butter a 9-inch cake pan and line the bottom with parchment paper.

In a large bowl, whisk the eggs and brown sugar until pale and smooth, about 1 minute. Add the sour cream, hoisin, vanilla, espresso powder, and ¾ teaspoon salt and whisk until smooth and incorporated.

Sift the flour, cocoa powder, baking powder, and baking soda directly into the bowl and whisk until just combined and smooth. Pour in the hot coffee and whisk until incorporated.

Pour the batter into the prepared pan, smooth the top with a spatula, and bake for 25 to 30 minutes, or until the cake starts to pull away from the sides and a toothpick inserted into the center comes out with only a few crumbs attached. Let cool in the pan on a rack for 20 minutes, then turn out of the pan onto the rack and allow to cool completely.

To make the frosting, use a handheld mixer (or a stand mixer fitted with the whisk attachment) on medium speed to whip the cream to soft peaks, 2 to 3 minutes, then add the cream cheese in 4 additions, beating for 10 to 15 seconds after each addition to incorporate. Add the confectioners' sugar, cornstarch, and vanilla and beat for 10 to 15 seconds, until incorporated and the frosting is smooth.

Frost the top of the cooled cake, using a knife or offset spatula to create generous swirls. Garnish with dark chocolate shavings (if you like), slice, and serve.

WHIPPED CREAM CAKE
à la Melba

SERVES 8 TO 10

I discovered peach melba as a teenager on a family trip to the South of France—one bite of the canned peach half with the zing of that raspberry sauce atop cool vanilla ice cream, and sixteen-year-old me was smitten. I was determined to eat it anytime it was on the menu for the remainder of the trip, and if that's not goals and commitment, I don't know what is. This is that experience in cake form (because cake makes everything better).

Whipped cream cake appears a few times in Grandma's recipe book. Grandma was a very practical person, so she no doubt loved the fact that it uses whipped cream in the cake for fat and lift, as well as in the topping. I've added Greek yogurt to the topping to stabilize it—you'll have glorious fluffy swirls for hours without weeping or losing volume.

CAKE

Unsalted butter, for the pan

2 cups all-purpose flour, plus more for the pan

2½ cups heavy cream, chilled

3 large eggs, at room temperature

1½ teaspoons vanilla extract or vanilla bean paste

1½ cups white sugar

2 teaspoons baking powder

Kosher salt

2 ripe but firm peaches, pitted and sliced

½ cup raspberries

RASPBERRY SAUCE

2 cups raspberries

¼ cup confectioners' sugar

1 teaspoon cornstarch

2 tablespoons fresh lemon juice

Kosher salt

TOPPING

¼ cup confectioners' sugar

¼ cup full-fat Greek yogurt

1 teaspoon vanilla extract

Place the bowl of a stand mixer in the fridge or freezer for 10 minutes. Preheat the oven to 350°F with a rack in the lower third of the oven. Butter and flour a 9-inch round cake pan and line with parchment paper.

Put the cream in the chilled mixer bowl and whip on medium-high speed for 3 to 4 minutes, or until stiff peaks form. Scoop out 2 cups of the whipped cream into a medium bowl, cover, and place in the fridge (this will be for the topping).

Add the eggs and vanilla to the whipped cream remaining in the mixer bowl and whip until just combined.

In a separate medium bowl, combine the flour, sugar, baking powder, and ½ teaspoon salt, then use a spatula to fold the dry ingredients into

(recipe continues)

In France, searching for Peach Melba

the cream mixture (the batter will be quite stiff). Pour the batter into the prepared pan and use a spatula or offset spatula to smooth and level the top. Bake for 60 to 65 minutes, or until a toothpick inserted into the center comes out clean. Let the cake cool completely in the pan on a wire rack.

Meanwhile, to make the raspberry sauce, put the raspberries in a blender and puree until smooth. Push the raspberry puree through a fine-mesh sieve into a small saucepan to remove the seeds. Whisk in the confectioners' sugar, cornstarch, lemon juice, and ⅛ teaspoon salt and bring to a simmer over medium-high heat. Turn the heat down to low and simmer for 2 to 3 minutes, until thickened. Transfer to a bowl, cover, and place in the fridge to cool and thicken slightly. (The sauce can be made a day in advance and stored in the fridge with plastic wrap pressed directly on the surface of the sauce to prevent a skin from forming.)

When the cake is cool, make the topping. Remove the reserved 2 cups whipped cream from the fridge, add the confectioners' sugar, Greek yogurt, and vanilla, and whisk until fully incorporated and stiff glossy peaks form, about 3 minutes.

To assemble, place the cake on a platter, dollop on the whipped cream topping, top with the peaches and raspberries, and drizzle with the raspberry sauce. Slice and serve.

Hot Tip Use canned or frozen peaches if fresh aren't available.

Remix! Top with lots of berries instead of peaches.

Another Remix! Make it tropical—top with chopped mango and pineapple and drizzle with honey.

LYCHEE LIME PAVLOVA

SERVES 8 TO 10

My mom remembers that in Macao during WWII (where the family temporarily relocated from Hong Kong), people would sell things from door to door, and one time Grandma bought a huge package of fresh lychees—quite the special treat during wartime. The family hugged the edges of the newspaper-lined table (to catch all the juice) and happily ate, gratefully peeling back the hard coral peel to reveal its creamy white fruit. This recipe features the fresh honeyed bite of lychees and a swirl of whipped cream, along with the meltingly tender crunch of meringue. It's a messily elegant grand gesture of a dessert, perfect for feeding a crowd gathered around any table (newspaper not required).

MERINGUE

¾ cup white sugar

5 large egg whites, at room temperature

Kosher salt

2 teaspoons cornstarch

1½ teaspoons white vinegar

½ teaspoon vanilla extract

½ teaspoon rose water

TOPPING

1 (20-ounce) can lychees, cut in half, plus 2 tablespoons syrup from the can

1 teaspoon white sugar

Grated zest of 2 limes, plus juice of 1 lime

1 cup heavy cream, chilled

1 tablespoon confectioners' sugar

1 teaspoon vanilla extract

1 tablespoon honey

Mint leaves, for garnish (optional)

Preheat the oven to 300°F.

Draw a 9-inch circle on a sheet of parchment paper, turn the parchment upside down, and place on a rimmed baking sheet.

To make the meringue, put the sugar in a food processor and pulse 10 to 12 times, until it is very fine.

In the bowl of a stand mixer fitted with the whisk attachment, combine the egg whites and ⅛ teaspoon salt and mix on low speed until the eggs are foamy and start to get fluffy. Increase the speed to high and beat until medium peaks form, 5 to 6 minutes. Slowly add the fine sugar, 1 tablespoon at a time, and whisk for 6 to 7 minutes, or until the mixture is glossy, smooth, and stiff.

Using a silicone spatula, gently fold in the cornstarch, vinegar, vanilla, and rose water. Mound the mixture onto the parchment in the center of the circle, then mold it into a round shape using the pencil lines as a guide. Use a spatula or offset spatula to create swirls and a very shallow dip in the middle. Place in the oven and immediately turn the oven temperature down to 250°F. Bake for 1 hour 15 minutes. Use a wooden spoon to prop the oven door ajar and allow the meringue to cool in the oven for 30 minutes. Remove from the oven and let cool completely.

In a small bowl, combine the lychees and syrup, white sugar, and lime juice and stir to combine. Set aside to macerate.

In the meantime, wipe the mixer bowl clean and fit with the whisk attachment. Add the cream and whip on medium speed until soft peaks form, about 2 minutes. Add the confectioners' sugar, vanilla, and zest of 1 lime and whip until stiff peaks form, about 1 minute. *(recipe continues)*

To assemble, transfer the meringue to a serving platter. If the meringue starts to crack, don't worry—just arrange the pieces on the platter. Top with the whipped cream, then use a slotted spoon to spoon the lychees atop. Drizzle with the honey, finish with the zest of the remaining lime, garnish with mint leaves (if using), and serve.

Hot Tip This recipe calls for canned lychees, but fresh lychees can also be used—simply peel, remove the pit, and cut in half. They are not as sweet as canned lychees, and since there will be no syrup from the can, add 1 tablespoon honey when macerating the lychees.

Remix! Replace the lychees with sliced strawberries, mango, or pineapple.

Mom (at left) and Grandma (third from left, back row) with the family circa late 1940s, Hong Kong.

DAN TAAT
PHYLLO TART

Dan taat is a dim sum favorite of mine—little bite-size (OK, perhaps two bites) tarts of flaky pastry filled with eggy custard—a very close cousin to Portuguese pasteis de nata—and the perfect end to a family lunch. As a kid I was known to eat a few too many at a time, much to the eyebrow-raising disapproval of Grandma (I usually ended up with a tummy ache, so Grandma was, again, correct). Here, I've used phyllo as a quick shortcut to creating a big sharing-size version, taking inspiration from Greek patsavouropita, where the phyllo is ruffled and swirled across the entire pie plate and the custard is poured atop all and baked for the ultimate family style dessert.

6 or 7 sheets phyllo dough, thawed

6 tablespoons unsalted butter, melted

½ cup sugar

½ cup evaporated milk, at room temperature

5 large eggs, at room temperature

1 teaspoon vanilla extract

Kosher salt

Preheat the oven to 350°F.

Cover the phyllo with a damp kitchen towel. Remove 1 sheet of phyllo and brush it with melted butter. Crunch up the long sides, gently form into a coil, and place in the center of a 9-inch deep-dish pie pan. Continue brushing the phyllo sheets with melted butter and forming the coil, handling the phyllo gently to create concentric circles. Make sure to not crush the phyllo too tightly—you'll want delicate, lofty coils. Use the last 2 sheets around the perimeter of the pie pan, creating a slightly raised border. Brush everything with melted butter. Bake for 15 to 18 minutes, or until pale golden brown.

Meanwhile, put the sugar in a medium bowl, add 1 cup hot water, and stir until the sugar is dissolved. Let cool, then whisk in the evaporated milk, eggs, vanilla, and ¼ teaspoon salt. Strain through a fine-mesh sieve into a clean bowl.

Pour the custard into the crust, ensuring it gets into all the crevices, and bake for another 20 to 25 minutes, or until the custard is set. Let cool for at least 10 minutes and serve warm or at room temperature.

Cardamom
MANGO PUDDING

SERVES 10 TO 12

I firmly believe that there are chocolate dessert people and fruit dessert people—I personally fall into the fruit dessert category. Mango is at the top of the heap for me as my most favorite fruit, so I knew I had to include it in this book. Mango pudding is a dim sum staple—a refreshing and light dessert that hits all those fruity dessert notes and is perfect after a big meal. I've added the floral peppery notes of cardamom and finished it off with a dash of Tajin, a nod to memories of the beach in Mexico, where vendors masterfully shower sweet, honeyed mango on a stick with Tajin's citrusy, salty spice kick.

5 Champagne or honey mangoes, divided

½ cup canned coconut cream, plus more for serving

1 teaspoon fresh lemon juice

¼ teaspoon ground cardamom

2 tablespoons unflavored gelatin

½ cup sugar

Kosher salt

Tajin or chili powder, for garnish (optional)

Peel, pit, and cube 3 of the mangoes. Use a food processor or blender to puree the mangoes until completely smooth. You will have about 2 cups. Add the coconut cream, lemon juice, and cardamom and pulse a few times to blend.

Pour 1½ cups hot water into a medium bowl, then sprinkle the gelatin atop and let sit for 1 minute. Stir a few times to combine, then whisk in the sugar and ¼ teaspoon salt until dissolved. Pour the mixture into the food processor and pulse until just combined.

Pour into a 9 x 13-inch baking dish, then tap the dish on the countertop a few times to pop any surface bubbles. Chill for at least 4 hours (there's no need to cover), or until set.

When ready to serve, peel, pit, and thinly slice the remaining 2 mangoes. To serve, cut squares of the pudding and transfer to individual shallow bowls, add a splash of coconut cream, garnish with sliced mango, and finish with a pinch of Tajin. Serve cold.

Hot Tip This can also be made in individual cups.

Really Hot Tip Note that Knox gelatin is not vegan, so if you or your guests have dietary requirements, use a vegan gelatin.

Remix! You can use frozen mango cubes (about 26 ounces) instead of fresh.

Brown Butter Miso
MOCHI BLONDIES

MAKES
24 SQUARES

You can find butter mochi on practically every corner in Hawaii—it's that ubiquitous because, well, it's that good. Mochi first landed in Hawaii with Japanese plantation workers in the 1800s, and while the exact origins of butter mochi are unknown, all I can do is give thanks that it exists. The tender bounce and chew, the lightness yet decadence from the butter—it's the perfect little snack, and very portable too, making it a great on-the-go treat. Grandma no doubt got her recipe from my auntie Florence, who moved to Hawaii in 1968 and is also an amazing cook in her own right (and incidentally the one who sparked my mom's love of cooking). For my version, I've browned the butter for a layer of toasted nutty flavor and added miso, which balances out the sweetness with its signature umami. A finish of flaky sea salt amps up the caramel notes of the brown butter and makes things not too sweet.

8 tablespoons (1 stick) unsalted butter, plus more for the pan

1 tablespoon white or yellow miso

5 large eggs

1 teaspoon vanilla extract

1 (12-ounce) can coconut cream

1½ cups white sugar

1½ cups dark brown sugar

1 pound sweet (glutinous) rice flour

1 tablespoon baking powder

½ teaspoon kosher salt

Flaky sea salt, for finishing

Preheat the oven to 350°F with a rack in the center position. Butter a 9 × 13-inch baking dish and line it with parchment paper, leaving a 1-inch overhang on the long sides.

In a small saucepan, melt the butter over medium heat and cook until golden nutty brown and fragrant, 5 to 6 minutes. Remove the pan from the heat and whisk in the miso (it won't completely dissolve but will ultimately get fully combined in later mixing—so don't stress!). Transfer to a large bowl and set aside to cool.

Once the butter miso mixture is cool, add the eggs, vanilla, coconut cream, white sugar, and dark brown sugar and mix until smooth. Add the sweet rice flour, baking powder, and kosher salt and mix until just combined.

Pour the batter into the prepared pan and bake for 50 to 60 minutes, or until deep golden brown with set edges and just the slightest wobble in the center.

Sprinkle lightly with flaky sea salt and cool completely, then use the parchment to lift out. Cut into 2-inch squares and serve.

Hot Tip Sweet rice flour is also known as mochiko flour or glutinous rice flour. I recommend Koda Farms, but any brand will do—most come in 1-pound boxes, which is what you need for this recipe.

A Plate of
VERY NICE ORANGES

SERVES 6 TO 8

There's comfort in oranges. A Chinese meal often ends with some very good fruit, usually the familiar happy hue of a plate of sliced orange wedges set down on the lazy Susan. It's the perfect palate-cleansing coda to an often big meal, and in my mind the correct order of things for any Chinese meal. Trust me, you'll miss them if they don't come out. I've added my own touches to this end-of-meal tradition—an easy sprinkle of five-spice sugar, a hit of lime zest and orange blossom water, and some flaky sea salt do their magic.

2 oranges, cut into wedges

2 teaspoons sugar

½ teaspoon five-spice powder

½ teaspoon orange blossom water

Grated zest of 1 lime

Flaky sea salt, for finishing

Arrange the orange wedges on a plate. In a small bowl, mix the sugar and five-spice and sprinkle atop the oranges. Finish with a drizzle of orange blossom water, sprinkle with lime zest and flaky sea salt, and serve.

Pineapple Croissant
BREAD PUDDING
with Suzette Sauce

SERVES 8 TO 10

Bread pudding must be one of the most low-lift but high-reward desserts out there—unapologetically unfussy, with a somewhat decent margin for error, it's rustic, comforting, delicious, and perfect for novice bakers. Now, you might be wondering what pineapple has to do with croissants, but hear me out. That bright, sweet, yet tart flavor profile, with those vanilla back notes, creates veritable little pockets of sunshine amid those buttery croissant layers. For the final flourish, I've taken a page from France again with a suzette sauce (of crêpes suzette fame) that adds a citrusy panache.

Unsalted butter, for the pan

8 croissants, sliced in half horizontally

6 large eggs

2 cups heavy cream

1 cup canned unsweetened coconut cream

⅔ cup sugar

1 tablespoon vanilla extract

1 tablespoon grated orange zest

1 teaspoon five-spice powder

Kosher salt

1 (20-ounce) can pineapple chunks, drained and chopped, juice reserved

Vanilla ice cream, for serving (optional)

SUZETTE SAUCE

8 tablespoons unsalted European-style butter

⅓ cup sugar

1 tablespoon grated orange zest

¼ cup fresh orange juice

¼ cup pineapple juice

Kosher salt

¼ cup Grand Marnier or Cointreau

If you have time, let the croissants sit out for 3 to 4 hours.

Preheat the oven to 375°F with a rack in the lower third of the oven. Butter a 3-quart casserole dish or 12-inch cast-iron skillet.

Arrange the sliced croissants in a tightly overlapping shingled fashion in the prepared casserole dish. Bake for 6 to 8 minutes, or until just toasted. Set aside to cool. Turn off the oven.

In a large bowl, whisk the eggs, heavy cream, coconut cream, sugar, vanilla, orange zest, five-spice, and ½ teaspoon salt. *(recipe continues)*

Add the pineapple to the croissants, making sure to tuck some in between the croissant slices and scattering the rest atop. Pour the custard over everything, gently press down with your hands to fully submerge the croissants, cover with aluminum foil, and set in the fridge for 1 to 2 hours.

Preheat the oven to 375°F.

Bake, covered, for 30 minutes, then uncover and bake for an additional 15 to 20 minutes, or until the custard is set and the pudding is puffed and deep golden brown.

When the bread pudding is nearly done, make the sauce. Combine the butter, sugar, orange zest and juice, pineapple juice, and ⅛ teaspoon salt in a small, heavy saucepan and stir over medium-low heat until the butter is melted and the ingredients are incorporated. Turn the heat down to low and simmer for 15 minutes, or until the sauce is thick and syrupy. Add the Grand Marnier carefully and slowly, then tilt the pan toward the burner flame to flambé the sauce (alternatively, use a long match or barbecue lighter). Let the flames die off, then stir and pour the sauce into a serving bowl or small jug.

To serve, scoop some bread pudding onto each dessert plate or shallow bowl, add a scoop of ice cream, if you like, and pour the warm sauce atop.

Fresh STRAWBERRY PIE
with Chamomile Miso Graham Cracker Crust

SERVES 6 TO 8

When I was growing up in Mill Valley, there was a highway-side restaurant called Hick'ry Pit (there is still one in the South Bay). I remember two things about it: The decor was high '70s walnut colonial with the waitresses straight out of Mel's Diner, and in the summer, they made a fresh strawberry pie. The in-season berries, all still whole, were piled up as high as a retro bouffant and enveloped in a bright red gelled glaze. We would always call ahead before going to pick one up, and on our way over I would be vibrating with excitement. On the way home, I'd always slide off the string, open the box carefully, and sneak one or two of the strawberries to eat. I've created my tribute to the Hick'ry Pit pie in slab form with bitter floral notes of jasmine tea in the no-bake crust. Serve with whipped cream, or do as I did as a kid and savor this treat unadorned.

CRUST

8 tablespoons unsalted butter

1 tablespoon yellow miso

½ cup whole raw almonds

12 graham crackers (1½ sleeves)

2 teaspoons chamomile tea leaves (about 2 tea bags)

¼ cup light brown sugar

Kosher salt

WHIPPED CREAM

2 cups heavy cream, chilled

2 tablespoons confectioners' sugar

1 teaspoon vanilla extract

STRAWBERRY FILLING

3 pounds strawberries, hulled and sliced

⅔ cup white sugar

3 tablespoons cornstarch

1 tablespoon fresh lemon juice

1 teaspoon vanilla extract

Kosher salt

To make the crust, melt the butter and miso in a small pot over medium heat, whisking to incorporate fully. (Alternatively, melt the butter and miso in a small bowl in the microwave for 1 to 2 minutes, then use a fork to mix.) Set aside to cool.

Toast the almonds in a dry pan over medium heat until fragrant, about 2 minutes. Transfer the almonds to a food processor and pulse until chunky. Add the graham crackers and tea leaves and process until well

(recipe continues)

blended. Add the butter–miso mixture, brown sugar, and ½ teaspoon salt and pulse to combine until the mixture resembles wet sand.

Press the mixture into a 9 × 13-inch baking dish or baking sheet with high sides, using the flat bottom of a glass or measuring cup to press the crumbs down evenly. Place in the fridge to set for at least 30 minutes or up to overnight.

Meanwhile, whip the cream with an electric mixer until soft peaks form, then add the confectioners' sugar and vanilla and continue to whip until stiff peaks form. Put the whipped cream in the fridge for at least 1 hour to set.

While the whipped cream is chilling, make the strawberry filling. Put 1 pound (about 4 cups) of the strawberries in a medium saucepan and use a potato masher or two forks to crush the strawberries—you should have small to medium chunks. In a small bowl, mix the white sugar and cornstarch until blended. Add the mixture to the saucepan, then turn the heat to medium. Add ½ cup boiling water, the lemon juice, vanilla, and ½ teaspoon salt and stir for 5 minutes, until the mixture thickens. Transfer to a large bowl, cover tightly, and place in the fridge to chill completely, at least 1 hour.

When ready to serve, remove the chilled crust, whipped cream, and strawberry filling from the fridge. Add the remaining sliced strawberries to the strawberry filling and gently toss so they are evenly coated, then spread the mixture evenly over the crust. Serve with the whipped cream. The pie is best served the day it's made.

Hot Tip Size matters! Look for smaller strawberries, which are usually sweeter.

Acknowledgments

THANK YOU . . .

It took more than a village to get this book done; it took a lifetime and more like a large town of people to help get this book off the ground. I feel so incredibly lucky to have found myself surrounded by kind, loving, and overall pretty freaking amazing people.

First off, the biggest thank-you to Helen Fong, my mom. Thank you for sharing your love of food with me, for your strength, for your humor. For seeing talent and drive in me before I could see it myself and for your steadfast, bedrock belief in every adventure I've embarked on. When I was designing runway collections, I often told people you were my muse, but now I realize you're my hero. I am who I am because of you.

To my family. What can I say? I quite literally could not have done it without you—thank you to Allen Fong for your wisdom. To my sister, Indigo Som, for being my cheerleader in life and the best big sister ever. To Rebecca Fong. A shout-out to my aunts (especially to Florence Wright-Holden for translating Grandma's notebook, Gloria Kwei, May Wang, and Katherine Woo), uncles, and cousins (special thanks to Eric Wright and Chia-Lien Wang) for sharing your recipes and memories of Grandma (and Grandpa), which were intrinsic to painting a fuller picture of her, and for reminding me of memories and recipes I'd completely forgotten! More than twenty years after her passing, and I feel like I had the honor to get to know Grandma all over again.

To Sarah Kwak and everyone at Harvest/Harper-Collins, thank you for believing that I had something unique and special to say and for truly seeing and championing my vision for *Family Style*.

To my agent, Cindy Uh (thank you, Eugene Han, for the intro!), and the team at CAA for guiding me through the process with such patience, thought, and understanding. It has been a journey (like, years!) and I'm thrilled to have been on it with you.

To my amazing photographer, Linda Xiao, for capturing everything I had dreamed about for so long in such beautiful photos—you "got me" from day 1. It was my honor to work with you—you led the ship with calm, kindness, and brilliance.

To the one and only Sue Li for bringing the food to life in the most exquisite way and for your cheerleading throughout the entire shoot. The energy you brought to set was unmatched.

To the wonderful and thoughtful Sarah Smart for amassing the perfect world of props, dishes, and more to reflect a world I truly want to dive into (and for sharing my 12th grade sense of humor, which made each day on set a blast).

To the amazing assistants at the photo shoot, Tommy McKiernan, Young Gun Lee, and Christina Zhang.

To Fatima Khajawa and Laura Manzano, for testing each and every recipe to make sure everything was just right. I learned so much from you both—thank you.

To Melissa Lotfy at Harvest for designing *Family Style* and making each and every page so stunningly beautiful.

To my team past and present! Eva Karagiorgas, Nicole Scharf, and Chloe Cardio at MONA Creative; Jennifer Sommer and Talia Summer at Sommerhouse; Ben Ayer at Benjamin Bellweather; and Nicole Esposito at White Spark.

To Doris Josovitz, for making such beautiful Lost Quarry plates and platters specially for the shoot at the eleventh hour.

To those who have buoyed me, tasted my food, tested my food, listened to me, advised me, and encouraged me, I am so lucky to have you all in my lives. Special shout-outs to my Silk Mafia—Marcus Teo, Rafe Totengco, Romy Chan, DB Kim, and Ron Laxamana; a big thank-you to Angie Mar for all the meals, wine, tears, and laughter; Rima Suqi for always being there for me, and for being a second pair of eyes for this cookbook; my dearly departed Pam Choy, I hope you're having our char siu and lots of leftovers in heaven and are proud of me; Christine Kim, Eddie Tawil, John Gregory, Danica Lo, Glenn Rosenberg, Jeffrey Cayle, Michael Paterson, Uli Wagner, Oberon Sinclair, Mohini Tadikonda, Andrew Lowenthal, Peter Bruce, and Andrew Tilbury for your sage and always correct advice. To Marina and Fran and Claire—we went through it

and we are out the other side—thank you for all the evenings of pasta and wine and friendship and so much more! To Jack and Salvador, Sara and Susan, China and Conor, and so many more. To Zac Young—the first person I told I wanted to write a cookbook—thank you for not laughing! A special shout-out to my home team Surfin Percy and crew, the best taste testers anywhere.

To Granny Heung Ong for not only your Chicken Essence but for your zest for life, which is a constant inspiration to me; your lifetime supply of homemade joong; and vegetables from your garden.

To Harry Som. Thank you for all your support over the years.

To my friends—new and old—in the food community who've embraced me and have been such a source of support and kindness. Special thanks to Kerry Diamond for all your support over the years.

And finally to Mary Woo. Grandma, you've been gone a long time—and it's funny that I can love you now even more than I did then. Thank you for being my guardian angel.

Universal Conversion Chart

OVEN TEMPERATURE EQUIVALENTS

250°F = 120°C   325°F = 160°C   400°F = 200°C   475°F = 240°C

275°F = 135°C   350°F = 180°C   425°F = 220°C   500°F = 260°C

300°F = 150°C   375°F = 190°C   450°F = 230°C

MEASUREMENT EQUIVALENTS

Measurements should always be level unless directed otherwise.

⅛ teaspoon = 0.5 mL

¼ teaspoon = 1 mL

½ teaspoon = 2 mL

1 teaspoon = 5 mL

1 tablespoon = 3 teaspoons = ½ fluid ounce = 15 mL

2 tablespoons = ⅛ cup = 1 fluid ounce = 30 mL

4 tablespoons = ¼ cup = 2 fluid ounces = 60 mL

5⅓ tablespoons = ⅓ cup = 3 fluid ounces = 80 mL

8 tablespoons = ½ cup = 4 fluid ounces = 120 mL

10⅔ tablespoons = ⅔ cup = 5 fluid ounces = 160 mL

12 tablespoons = ¾ cup = 6 fluid ounces = 180 mL

16 tablespoons = 1 cup = 8 fluid ounces = 240 mL

Index

Note: Page references in *italics* indicate photographs.